Double Acts

Double Acts

A Modern History
of Tottenham
in 10½ Strike
Partnerships

Julie Welch

FOOTBALL
SHORTS

FOOTBALL SHORTS

Series curator Ian Ridley

First published by Pitch Publishing
and Floodlit Dreams, 2024

Floodlit Dreams

Pitch Publishing
9 Donnington Park,
85 Birdham Road,
Chichester, West Sussex,
PO20 7AJ
www.pitchpublishing.co.uk
info@pitchpublishing.co.uk

A CIP catalogue record is available for this book
from the British Library.

ISBN 978 1 80150 669 4

Cover by Steve Leard
Typesetting and origination by Pitch Publishing
Printed and bound in India by Replika Press Pvt. Ltd.

Prologue

Tottenham Hotspur Stadium, 19 May 2021
It's the last-but-one game of the weirdest season in living memory, against Aston Villa. In March 2020 football was suspended as Covid took hold, and on its resumption was played behind closed doors in front of empty seats, fans getting their fix from televised games with a soundtrack of canned crowd noise. From a Spurs point of view, the weirdness has been intensified by the return of Gareth Bale from Real Madrid for a swansong and the sacking of José Mourinho six days before the League Cup Final. Ryan Mason's first task as interim manager was to preside over defeat to Manchester City at Wembley.

Since then, though, he has been working on the mood of a demoralised, disaffected squad. 'Imagine telling a Spurs fan in 2015 that our manager in 2021 would be Ryan Mason and Gareth Bale would be the first person to score under his tenure,' the writer Jack Kirby-Lowe tweeted after Spurs collected three points on Sunday against Wolves at home. Now they are hoping for three more today to clinch a place in next season's Europa League. Some chance. Steven Bergwijn scores a wonderful opening goal, winning the ball up top, holding off two challenges and half-volleying into the top right corner from just outside the box. Nobody else is looking up for it today, though; Eric Dier's decision-making is off-kilter, Harry Winks seems discombobulated, Pierre-Emile Højbjerg is passing as though he's been made to wear snow shoes, and Sergio Reguilón is having a nightmare: a sliced own goal and failed clearances allowing Ollie Watkins to score the winner with a low finish beyond Hugo Lloris after holding off Dier's challenge.

A place in Europe, though, isn't the big item on everyone's wish list. You suspect, in fact, that the vast majority would sacrifice a top-six finish for a favourable answer to their annual prayers. Now, with 10,000 finally back in the stadium as Covid restrictions are eased, a chant rises up from the terraces:

PROLOGUE

Harry Kane, Harry Kane, Harry Kane,
We want you to stay.

It's a theme that has been familiar for far too many seasons. Is this year going to be Kane's last at Spurs? The gloom has been intensified by Kane's latest announcement. He wants to leave this summer, and it's no secret which club he'll leave for if it's allowed to happen. Eye-watering sums have been mentioned: anything from £150m upwards to let him go, but for Manchester City's gazillionaire owners, that's practically loose change.

As the final whistle goes, Kane enfolds Son Heung-min in a long and solemn embrace. It looks far too much as though he's saying a final farewell. Is this it, then? The end of Kane and Son, the finest strike partnership in the land?

I once asked Lawrie McMenemy, the old Saints manager, if he thought a strike partnership was like a marriage. 'A marriage is for life,' he scoffed, thus managing to be wrong and right all at once because a lot of marriages are not for life but nor are strike partnerships. If you're lucky you get two or three years out of the pairing before it all starts to go brown at the edges, and one of the pair finds someone else, gets a better offer, walks out when you don't expect it. Jürgen Klinsmann and Teddy Sheringham were one of the best Spurs duos of all time and they lasted only a season before their parting of ways.

But while they're working as a pair, few sights in football can match them. These are players with supreme football intelligence, who have a picture of what's going on around them, can make the right decision in a fraction of a second, and have the technical ability to execute it. 'With a great strike partnership, you have to concentrate all the time,' says Gary Mabbutt, looking at it from a defender's point of view. 'Most partnerships need three or four seconds to set up. The great ones need one second, so if you stop concentrating for longer than that, they're in.' Describing them like this, though, spoils the magic. As Theo Delaney, producer and presenter of the podcast *Life Goals*, puts it, 'You can see that two individuals working *together*, in tandem, the one enhancing the other, can achieve wonderful things. When you see it happen beautifully on the pitch it fills you with joy and happiness.'

Part of the sense of wonder generated comes from that apparently telepathic knowledge of where the other guy is. How do they do it? Even Jimmy Greaves, who with Bobby Smith and then Alan Gilzean formed two of the greatest duos in Spurs history, couldn't supply an answer to the mystery. 'You don't practise it and you can't coach it,' he said. 'You certainly can't do any of the things coaches would have you believe. With Gilly, it wasn't like that at all. It's just something that happens – it comes together from time to time and it works, it sparks and it's great.'

There's another point to be made here: if I was going to tell the Spurs story through the medium of strike partnerships, which ones would I choose? Some were part of sides that brought the club glory, so they picked themselves. Greaves had two successful partnerships, with Bobby Smith and then Gilzean; before Greaves came along, Smith and Les Allen were the pair who helped win the Double. After that were Gilzean and Martin Chivers, and then came Steve Archibald and Garth Crooks. All these partnerships were formed in the days of 4-4-2, a time when there were no databases, tracking monitors and spreadsheets, and no one talked about 'assists', an Americanism I loathe while acknowledging its usefulness. I'm just glad it wasn't around when Smith and Allen were operating, and when practically every player in the 1960/61 side was helping each other to score goals. I'd never want the romance of the Double reduced to mere totting up.

Back then, pretty much every team was set up in the 4-4-2 formation. In its simplest form, you had the big lump to head it down, and the little one to run in and score. Sometimes there'd be a 4-3-3 with wingers, or overlapping full-backs, but that was about as sophisticated as it got and Alf Ramsey's England were derided as 'wingless wonders' almost to the moment they won the World Cup. In the excellent book *The 90-Minute Manager*, authors David Bolchover and Chris Brady quote George Burley, the one-time manager of Southampton: 'If I could choose any players in the world to make up my team I would go for a 4-4-2,' which Burley said 'gave the greatest number of attacking options with the most solid defensive shape'. But by the time that book came out in 2002, the game had already started to evolve.

'As football became a science rather than a sport,' says Spurs commentator Daniel Wynne, 'it was all about formations, about trying to catch out your opponent.' In the case of Spurs, this sea change could be traced back to a point just after the mid-1980s, when David Pleat introduced his five-man midfield with Clive Allen as the singleton up front. In case you were wondering why this book features 10½ partnerships, Clive Allen is the half. Nico Claesen was brought in to be his other half but ended up as the wallflower.

In a way, Allen's amazing season adumbrated the end of the old type of strike partnership. Gary Lineker, for example, was at his deadliest in tandem with Paul Gascoigne, a midfielder (if you can call Gazza anything as mundane as that). Klinsmann and Sheringham were actually part of the Famous Five, which started as Ossie Ardiles's ultimately doomed attempt to recreate Brazil in 1970 before Gerry Francis came along and hosed it down a bit. As with the earlier partnerships, Klinsmann and Sheringham were an easy choice to make. After that, though, it became more difficult. Both Spurs' most recent trophies (and admittedly 'recent' is doing a lot of reaching here) were won with goals not scored by recognised strike duos. The winner of the 2008 League Cup, for instance, went in off the face of Jonathan Woodgate, a centre-back. When Spurs won the League Cup in 1999, the only goal was scored by the midfielder Allan Nielsen. Among a group of underperforming or mediocre strikers around the time of that trophy, Les Ferdinand stood out as a player who had some class, except he wasn't picked for the final. In the end I focussed on the previous season, when Spurs were largely concreted into the relegation zone. It was a returning Klinsmann, with Ferdinand as his sidekick, who got Spurs out of their fix, and I decided that pairing deserved inclusion because they diverted the course of the club's history in a positive direction when it looked as if things were heading for disaster.

This brings me on to partnerships that I haven't given whole chapters to because of constrictions on space. I deliberated almost to the extent of losing sleep about whether or not to include Dimitar Berbatov and Robbie Keane. Keane was a lovely player for Spurs and scored some great goals (and turned some great cartwheels), but I always looked on Berbatov as a standalone player, an individualist rather than one half of a twosome. There might also have been a residue of pique at his boarding a plane to Manchester *actually on transfer deadline day* in September 2008.

It was also limitations of space that precluded my devoting a whole chapter to the fantastic one-night stand that was Lucas Moura and Dele Alli in Amsterdam in 2019. That season Spurs reached the Champions League Final with a squad running on fumes, depleted by injuries to key figures including, for a big part of it, Harry Kane. It was the apogee of Pochettino's Spurs, and in a few months he was replaced by Mourinho. Which brings me back more or less to where I started: the summer of 2021. Mourinho might have left, but Kane didn't go to Manchester City in the end. The Kane and Son partnership wasn't over yet. Not by a long chalk, as we will see.

* * *

As ever, I'm grateful for the observations, anecdotes and insights of fellow Spurs fans Theo Delaney, Chris Slegg, Toby Benjamin, Daniel Wynne,

Gareth Dace, Alan Fisher and Ivan Cohen. Ivan was one of the fans whose recollections featured in *81: The Year That Changed Our Lives*, the book I wrote in collaboration with Steve Perryman about Tottenham's fantastic season that finished in FA Cup triumph. Ivan is now Emeritus Professor of Finance at Richmond University, but at the time of the semi-final against Wolves at Hillsborough he was a Sheffield University student who rocked up at the team hotel with a group of fellow Spurs eggheads, to which end he told me a superb story involving Keith Burkinshaw and Steve Archibald. The punchline contained profanities that had to be removed when our book came to be approved by Tottenham Hotspur, thus rendering the anecdote incomplete. It is included here in full.

There are three blogs and podcasts I've been grateful for while writing this: Alan Fisher's eloquent and knowledgeable *Tottenham On My Mind*, *The Spurs Show* (thank you, as ever, Mike Leigh) and Theo Delaney's *Life Goals*. As for books, Chris Slegg's *The Team That Dared To Do*, in collaboration with Gerry Francis, is a riveting record of the 1994/95 season that started so alarmingly but was transmogrified by one of the most jaw-dropping transfer coups in the history of football, and *Is Gascoigne Going To Have A Crack?* by Gareth Dace is a fascinating account of an overlooked decade in Spurs history, the 1990s. For anyone writing about Spurs, Bob Goodwin's *Tottenham Hotspur: The Complete Record* is an essential (and in my case much-thumbed) reference guide, and Ivan Ponting's *Tottenham Hotspur Player by Player* is full of lovingly compiled player portraits.

For the early history of Spurs strike partnerships my main source was the *Daily Telegraph*. It was the paper I grew up with and its football coverage back in the late 1950s and early 1960s was far more extensive than anything else Fleet Street had to offer. One thing I'd forgotten when I returned to it decades later was the way that, instead of being on the back pages where you'd expect it to be, the football was four or five pages in, cushioned from the front by classified ads for anything from Situations Vacant to lawnmowers and nylons. Be that as it may, I spent many happy hours at the British Library, winding reels of microfilm from the time of my childhood and teens – from October

1958, when Bill Nicholson became Spurs manager, through to April 1961, where I finally uncovered the report I was looking for: that of the night Spurs clinched the title and with it the first half of the Double, with Smith and Allen each providing a goal. If this book was going to be a history of Spurs told through strike partnerships, then here was Strike Partnership Zero.

Strike Partnership Zero

Smith and Allen

17 April 1961: White Hart Lane on an overcast evening. Spurs had left it pretty late to clinch the title, as far as the fans were concerned anyway. This was a game they were expected to win without getting their hair messed up, but instead they were one down most of the way through the first half, from a free kick awarded to Sheffield Wednesday just outside the box and a goal by Don Megson. After that they hammered for a long time at Wednesday's locked and bolted door; almost three-quarters of an hour of grappling, shirt-tugging and shin-hacking endured, with half-time nearly up when the best strike force in the league turned it into the night of nights.

'SMITH PIERCES WALL OF STEEL' punned the *Daily Express*; 'SMITH AND ALLEN CLINCH VICTORY

IN INSPIRED TWO MINUTES', said the *Daily Telegraph*, and really that was all you needed to know, except that it started with a classic bit of Terry Dyson (the shortest player on the field by several inches), as he beat Peter Swan (the tallest) to Peter Baker's clearance and headed the ball into the goal area. Bobby Smith, wearing two Wednesday defenders as accessories, flicked the ball over another one's head: right foot, left foot, *blam*, a volley into the roof of the net. When Smith's goal went in, the first team-mate to run towards him was Les Allen.

And Wednesday just went like a piece of snapped elastic. Another free kick, this time in Tottenham's favour. Danny Blanchflower signalled Maurice Norman to move up and the usual perfect placement followed, right on to Norman's head. Norman nodded it sideways and Allen hooked it waist-high past Ron Springett. And this time Smith ran towards Allen.

Out there in the rest of the world Yuri Gagarin had just become the first man in space, Elizabeth Taylor was winning her Best Actress Oscar for *BUtterfield 8* and 1,400 Cuban exiles were landing in the Bay of Pigs in a doomed attempt to overthrow

Fidel Castro, but in this part of north London even the second coming would have made no impact. The Park Lane and the Paxton ends were emptying on to the pitch, sprinting towards the directors' box, chanting 'We want Danny! We want Danny!' The whole team gathered in the directors' box, which brought a roar even Gagarin might have heard if he'd cupped his ears. There were fans with flares on the end of poles, Les Allen hanging over the edge of the box and waving a bath towel for a banner, people clambering in to hug their heroes. Blanchflower didn't speak, for a change. This was a team affair; everyone had to share the glory.

It hadn't always been Smith and Allen. Five years previously, Bobby Smith was a striker in search of a partner; the pairing up front had been Smith and A.N. Other. Wind back the reel to the 1955/56 seasons. Yes, that really was Spurs in the relegation zone. When Bobby Smith signed that December, Tottenham Hotspur were one place off the bottom of the table, with their 1951 title win a receding memory. Their great game-changing manager Arthur Rowe had been discarded by the club due to his mental health breakdown, and his

19

replacement – the one-club man Jimmy Anderson – had been promoted above his competence and was at odds with Blanchflower. While Anderson failed to cut it in the dug-out, though, there was one area in which he was smart: he couldn't half spot a player. Ron Henry, Peter Baker, Terry Dyson and Cliff Jones were all his recruits. Maurice Norman arrived from East Anglia in November 1955, and no more than a month later came another part of the Double side-to-be.

Bobby Smith had come down to London in 1950 from his Yorkshire village. An ironstone miner's son for whom Middlesbrough was the metropolis, Smith had been playing for his local Redcar club when Chelsea snapped him up. You would have to hang around a long time before you confused Lingdale in the North Riding with Sloane Square and the King's Road and, 17 years old and fazed by the change of environment, Smith fled home for a while before giving the big city another try. Finding his feet at Stamford Bridge, he exploded into action with 18 goals in 48 top-tier games in his first two seasons as a pro. Even so, by the late summer of 1955 his progress had stalled. It made no difference that he scored four times in seven games once the new season opened; by the time winter had set in he was a Tottenham man.

You couldn't say the fans were bowled over from the off. Smith, they opined, was unworthy of the Spurs shirt. They expected flair and he had arrived at White Hart Lane with the reputation of a bulldozing front man, mullering defenders and merrily dishing it out before it got dished out to him. As Jimmy Greaves was later to observe, 'Smithy didn't think he was in the game until he'd hammered into the goalkeeper in the earliest possible moment in the match.' In those early days, no one realised he was capable of guile and finesse when it mattered, a thug with a side-hustle as an artist, or maybe it was the other way round.

Smith had been brought in by Anderson as an upgrade on the frustrating Alfie Stokes, a local lad who came to attention playing for non-league Clapton. Stokes had the kind of looks that fifty years later would have swept him into any boy band, and for a while gave the impression of having the same sort of stardust in his boots, scoring on his debut against Bolton and troubling the keeper twice for

England Under-23s in his first international. That wasn't the whole story, though. The dazzling first-half performances were frequently followed up by 45 minutes when he just ran out of juice.

Not that Spurs were short of alternatives. Just look at the scorers in the run of league games starting with Smith's debut:

24 December, Spurs 2 Luton Town 1: Robb, Duquemin
26 December, Spurs 4 West Bromwich Albion 1: Norman, Brooks (pen), Duquemin 2
27 December, West Bromwich Albion 1 Spurs 0
31 December, Spurs 2 Charlton Athletic 1: Duquemin, Robb
14 January, Arsenal 0 Spurs 1: Robb

That tells you something. Smith didn't find the net till the end of January, in the 1-1 home draw with Everton. By the end of the season, his tally had risen to 12, bulked up by a final-day hat-trick against Sheffield United, but even then his perfect match was a long way off. Over the next few seasons the hope was that Johnny Brooks would be The

One. Brooks had glamour. He was one of the first footballers in Britain to advertise shampoo, putting his name and handsome head of curls to Max Factor For Men. There was no doubt he was very buff and he was also a gifted footballer: superb touch, brilliant dribbler, all the bells and whistles. On the minus side, he never really fancied it when faced with defenders who were more likely to break his legs than rumple his hair.

And what about Len Duquemin, the chunky warhorse who had led the line when Spurs claimed the top prize in 1951? Yep, still there in 1957. Dave Dunmore had been signed as his replacement, but Duquemin wasn't having that and fought him off the same as he'd fought off Stokes. Smith and Dunmore didn't gel either. There was Tommy Harmer in the number 8 shirt, of course, but he did his own thing. In fact, if anybody was Smith's partner back then, it was the outside-left, George Robb. An Arthur Rowe signing, Robb was fast approaching heirloom status but he still had goals in him and, more importantly for Smith, he provided the assists.

The 1955/56 season had ended with Spurs too close to the drop zone for comfort. Things were on the up, though, for them and for Smith. In 1956/57, they finished second. In the 1957/58 season they ended up third, with a side augmented by the arrival from Swansea that February of the flying winger Cliff Jones, and Smith on a roll. His 36 goals – including five braces and three hat-tricks as well as the four that battered Aston Villa – equalled the record set by George Harper in 1931, when Spurs were a second-tier side.

With that in mind, 1958/59 was supposed to be the season they won the title, but instead it was time for Spurs to undergo one of their periodic spells of turmoil. Cliff Jones broke his leg in pre-season in a tackle by Peter Baker; Blanchflower fell out with Jimmy Anderson again; and August yielded no points at all, a sudden dead zone. September and the start of October weren't much better either and, as autumn set in, Jimmy Anderson – by now running on empty – stood down.

11 October 1958. If this is a history of modern Spurs, that's when it really started. The team only found out 15 minutes before kick-off against Everton that Bill Nicholson, their brusque, razor-haired wing-half-turned-coach, was now top man.

The scoreline that day was bonkers: 10-4 to the Lilywhites. In all their days, Tottenham Hotspur had never come away with double figures in a league match. 'HARMER INSPIRATION OF GOAL RIOT' was the *Daily Telegraph* headline:

'No one benefited more than Smith, who scored four, and Robb, who looked like the star winger he was a few seasons ago. As a result, Everton were in trouble from the third minute when Stokes put Spurs in front. Though Jimmy Harris hit back with a fifth-minute goal for Everton, nothing could stop Harmer and his men from sweeping comfortably into a 6-1 lead by half-time...'

By then, of course, the contest was pretty well killed off. Smith scored four in all. Even a defender, John Ryden, hit the back of the net. Everton were that bad. If you're Spurs, you probably know about Harmer's warning to Nicholson afterwards: 'We don't score ten every game.' 'It can only get worse from here,' Blanchflower added, and he wasn't wrong. Smith carried on banging them in, but often they were consolation goals that went along with defeats. From 22 November to 13 December, they came away with a solitary point from seven league games. Between the end of January and the start of March they notched up two points in five. Saved from the drop largely by Smith scoring four against West Bromwich Albion in the penultimate game, they finished up fifth from bottom.

One good thing did happen towards the end of that season. Click, click, click: Nicholson, the great assembler of human components, was putting together the Double team. Dave Mackay made his debut in March 1959, though nobody got a glimpse of what that would mean at first since, ruled out by a foot injury, he didn't reappear till that August. By then, Nicholson had added John White. There was only one more piece to slot into place – a strike partner for Bobby Smith.

Imagine the carry-on if this were Nicholson trying to sign a striker today. It would go on for months. In contrast, the process that took Les Allen from Chelsea to Spurs took all of a couple of weeks, in addition to which it cost Spurs nothing. He was 22 and had been on Chelsea's books since his teens but – upstaged by a wonderkid called Jimmy Greaves – had spent most of his time in the reserves. Nicholson had been keeping track of him, though, and liked the look of him. A wasted talent, in his opinion: a bit on the slow side but good at sniffing out chances and a reliable finisher. Even then, Nicholson was to claim he didn't set out to get him. Everything was initiated by Ted Drake, Chelsea's manager. In spite of Greaves, Chelsea were floundering and Drake thought Johnny Brooks would be the answer to his prayers. Nicholson's response to Drake was damning: 'What do you want him for? He's not the kind of player who will get you out of a hole.' Drake persisted, and that was it – a straight swap, with the despised glamour boy going one way and the underused unknown going the other.

'I went into training as normal and got called in,' said Allen. 'Ted Drake said, "I'd like you to go to Tottenham," and I said, "Why?" "I'm doing a deal with them and they've asked for you." I was flabbergasted. I didn't know what to think. Tottenham were a bigger club than Chelsea. We met Bill Nick in Ilford where my dad used to work. He was a very clever man, Bill. He picked John White out, Dave, Bill Brown. "You're the last piece in the jigsaw," Bill said. "I've been watching you. I admired the way you scored against us." That was it. Johnny went that way and I went this way. The next day I was training with Tottenham.'

A burly, frowning, shy lad, Allen was there to give the attack more bite, but the impression was that he felt undermined at first by a sense of inferiority in that team of stars. Blanchflower, Mackay, Jones, White – all world-class talent. Smith wasn't far behind. The late David Lacey of *The Guardian* once saw two blokes having a punch-up on the terraces at White Hart Lane over who was the better striker, Smith or Brian Clough. That was one of the afternoons when Smith scored a hat-trick, which could have settled the argument. Even the uncapped players in that side would have been welcomed with a brass band and bunting by any other team in the country. Terry Medwin and Mel Hopkins were internationals and they were playing in the stiffs. As Blanchflower said of Allen: 'He looked careworn before his time. It was only when he was picked for the England Under-23 side that we realised how young he was.'

In lifestyle and personality, these strike partners were pretty much opposites. Smith was a bit of a naughty boy. He lived the life: boozers, the ladies and, above all, bookies. When I say Bobby liked a bet, he *really* liked a bet. Allen, in contrast, was a family man, cautious, unshowy, matter-of-fact. 'He was a second centre-forward for us,' Blanchflower wrote later, 'with an unobtrusive style for scoring goals – a silent killer. He was always better than he appeared to be.'

The 1959/60 season was when Tottenham should have done the Double but didn't (it's a Spurs trope, that). The new strike partnership debuted on 19 December against Newcastle United and drew a blank, but a week later Allen stuck two in the net in the 4-2 win away to Leeds. Two days into 1960, he scored the winner at Birmingham City. A fortnight later, he and Smith did for Arsenal between them – 3-0, Allen getting two of the goals. The week after that, Smith's two goals did for Manchester United. At that point the Double seemed a real prospect, even if a 2-2 draw away to Crewe Alexandra in the FA Cup fourth round was a reality check: 'CREWE SHOW UP SPURS' LIMITATIONS' intoned the *Daily Telegraph*, grudgingly conceding 'Spurs may or may not win the League Championship but judging by their efforts at Crewe the Double is beyond them.' The replay, of course, is part of folklore, a spectacular display of Tottenham's strike force: a 13-2 rout delivered in front of an audience of 64,365, with so many goals that in the end you almost lost count. The only forward who didn't score that night was John White, for a change. Smith got four but Allen outdid him with five, a defining night for him – proof that he was no longer a nonentity but very much Smith's equal partner. Meanwhile, the *Daily Telegraph* reporter had to perform a rapid reverse ferret: 'Spurs sounded an unmistakeable warning at White Hart Lane last night that nothing and nobody will be allowed this season to stop them pulling off footballing's dream – the double of League Championship and F.A. Cup.'

This was Spurs, though. Drawn at home to Blackburn Rovers in the fifth round, their opponents put three past them and *pfft*, the Double was gone. As for the title, that wasn't going to happen either. The game that might have made the difference is another one that has gone down in folklore: Spurs v Manchester City, 16 April 1960. In the closing microseconds of the first half, Tottenham won a penalty for handball. Bert Trautmann saved Cliff Jones's spot kick but Jones tapped in the rebound. His goal was disallowed. The referee had added just enough time for the penalty to be taken and had blown the whistle the moment Trautmann had made the save. In the second half, City scored the only goal of the game, effectively putting the kibosh on Tottenham's title hopes. That's the legend, anyway. If the referee hadn't blown his whistle... If City hadn't scored... In football, there's always an 'if'.

At the end of August 1960, Smith scored a hat-trick against Blackpool that meant he had scored more goals than any other Spurs player ever, overtaking the record 138 set by George Hunt back in the 1930s. A lot more were on their way. In the Cup semi-final at Villa Park the following April, Spurs beat Burnley 3-0, Smith providing two of the goals. The Spurs fans carried him off the pitch. Fast-forward to the Wembley final and 6 May 1961. Much better games had happened that season, everyone was agreed on that, but they did it. Smith opened the scoring, Dyson added the second. It would have been good for Allen to get on the scoreboard but he played a key part too, though not in the way he would have preferred; in the 19th minute his freak tangle of legs with Len Chalmers left the Leicester right-back a hobbling passenger for the rest of the afternoon, which didn't do much for the spectacle.

Anyway, that was it – the Double done, the century's biggest challenge in football completed. All the joy is there in the photos: Allen and Mackay on the pitch, grinning, arms linked; the obligatory gathering in the communal bath, stark naked but accessorised by the odd glass of beer; the open-top bus parade along the High Road, Allen on the front row with Smith at his shoulder. Records had gone tumbling: 11 wins on the bounce at the start of the season – best in Football League history; unbeaten in the first 16 games; 31 wins in 42 games; 16 away wins; only 17 players used; 50 points from only 29 games – all First Division records, with 66 points and 33 from away games equalling the Arsenal record set 30 years back. Smith's goal tally was 28 in the league and five in the Cup. Allen's was close to matching it, with 23 in the league and four in the Cup.

And it still wasn't enough. Who would have guessed – who could possibly have imagined as they celebrated on the Wembley pitch that May afternoon – that an axe was about to be driven through the partnership?

Three's a Crowd

Greaves and Smith

White Hart Lane, 16 December 1961

It's one of the coldest days of winter so far, the kind of day you wouldn't want to be outdoors, but the terraces at White Hart Lane are jam-packed. Jimmy Greaves's first league game for Tottenham, against Blackpool, is about to happen and the boy is box office; even his run-out for Spurs reserves away to Plymouth Argyle a few days earlier gave Home Park a record reserve-fixture attendance of 12,907. Now, with 38 minutes about to tick up on the clock, Dave Mackay makes one of his trademark long throw-ins. This one is from the left, and Terry Medwin flips a header back. Twisting, airborne, Greaves whacks the shot almost over his shoulder into Tony Waiters' net. By the time Waiters is picking himself up off the goalmouth mudslick, Greaves is already invisible under a pile of white shirts, as though he's been part of this team for ever.

This celebratory pile-up after Greaves's debut goal at White Hart Lane answered the question that had nagged away at him – how his new team-mates would accept him. He had been alerted to potential discord when John Smith, the reserve-team player, had greeted his entrance into the away dressing room at Plymouth Argyle with: 'Here she is.' *Oh hello,* thought Greaves, *here we go.* He was going to have to do a bit of work to prove himself. Nor did it help when, as he ran on to the Home Park pitch, Argyle's chairman had drawn attention to him by seizing the microphone and welcoming him back from Italy on behalf of Plymouth Argyle, Devon, Cornwall and the whole of England. Now, though, Greaves knows everyone has accepted him, and it gets even better. Two minutes later Mackay's at it again, this time floating a cross in towards the far post. Greaves back-pedals a couple of feet and finds the only empty space in the crowded goalmouth in which to nod the ball home. Then, midway through the second half, he gets the jump on everyone else from Les Allen's corner kick. Another nod past

Waiters, a hat-trick on his debut. Spurs win 5-2. Job done.

Jimmy Greaves was a one-off, a player of the stature of Messi or Cruyff, impossible to replicate. This isn't to belittle Bobby Smith or Les Allen, but no other English striker could measure up to his spontaneity, his seemingly magic ability to be in the right place at the right time, or the almost impudent snatching-up of opportunities that no one else had spotted. Fans who never saw him at his magic best, fans who weren't born when he was in his prime, still revere him. Even people who weren't that interested in football knew who he was, whether it was as the 'teenage sensation' eulogised on the sports pages in those early days or, when it looked as though he was about to head off to AC Milan, allegedly trousering a massive signing-on fee, the spoilt young brat of English football.

Most young players improve incrementally, season upon season – Harry Kane, struggling as a 20-year-old to make his mark as a loanee at Leicester City in the Championship, is a golden example. Kane had to *work* to become Harry Kane. In the case of Greaves, though, you had the same sort of feeling as you did some 20 years on with Glenn Hoddle. It was the realisation that everything was there right from the beginning – ball skills, positional awareness, absolute confidence in his ability. In Greaves's first season there were 22 goals in 27 appearances. In the 1959/60 season, his 29 goals were what kept Chelsea from the drop zone. Between 1957 and 1961, in fact, he scored 124 in 157 games. On 19 November 1960, when he registered a hat-trick against Manchester City, one of those goals was his 100th in the league, making him the youngest ever player to press that button. Years later, playing alongside Greaves as a youngster just coming into the first team, Steve Perryman was amazed by him: 'It was his balance, his off-the-mark sharpness, his eye for goal. I saw him score some unbelievable ones in training, in five-a-side, with hockey-size goals. When you see Messi when he's on a run, flicking through people – that's how Jimmy was.'

There wasn't much TV coverage back then. If you weren't there for a lot of Greaves's goals, you had to imagine them because the cameras weren't there either. They weren't at White Hart Lane in

1957 when he scored on another debut – this one as a spiky-haired boy in baggy shorts and a Chelsea shirt. It was the kind of goal he seemed to score at will, the first of many, springing himself from three defenders before stroking the ball into the net. A few years later, Les Allen held that up as a shining example to his young son Clive: 'Look at Jimmy, look how he passes it into the goal.' Seeing what he did that day in 1957, Bill Nicholson was a man smitten: 'It had all the hallmarks of his game, improvisation and genius. I had to have him.' For Nicholson, having Smith and Allen, the best strike partnership in the league, was no longer enough. After all, 1961/62 was supposed to be the season Spurs won the Treble: the league and the FA Cup *and* the European Cup.

The beginning of the end of the Smith–Allen partnership went back to the spring of 1961. Four days before the duo sealed the title with that two-minute goal storm against Sheffield Wednesday and sent Tottenham storming towards the Double, the page lead in the *Daily Telegraph* was: 'GREAVES MAY GET £20,000 SIGNING FEE: TRANSFER TO COST MILAN £100,000'. The Italian league was on the brink of lifting its ban on foreign players, and the press were treating it as a done deal. Chelsea fans who had been telling themselves the departure of their best player couldn't possibly be happening were now faced with the truth: 'After days of silence, Chelsea yesterday admitted that they had agreed to let Greaves go to Milan. Their chairman, Mr Joe Mears, who has just returned from holiday, said a five-figure fee had already been deposited in their bank.'

You could hardly blame Greaves. He was playing in an inexperienced side with an eggshell defence and he knew he wasn't going to win anything with Chelsea any time soon. But for someone whose talent lay in being in the right place at the right time, Greaves's move to AC Milan was pretty much the polar opposite. The place was all wrong and the timing lamentable. Shortly after his departure to Italy the British restrictions on players' wages were abandoned, thanks to the campaign fought by players' representative Jimmy Hill. From then on there would only be a minimum wage. Greaves could have bettered himself by staying in England. Instead he was stuck far from home, knowing that he'd signed up to a life that was never going to work for him. Milan's Nereo Rocco was a martinet coach who monitored Greaves's every move. Worse than that was the system in which he was expected to play: *catenaccio*, which placed defensive invulnerability over attacking flair. The lack of freedom on and off the pitch triggered a plunge into depression for someone who, in his own words, liked to 'just get in as close as I can and let rip'.

That summer he escaped briefly back to England for a football function at the Café Royal. You can't help suspecting that fellow guest Bill Nicholson was waiting for his moment and, when he spotted Greaves heading for the gents, nipped in alongside him. 'You should have gone somewhere better than Milan,' he said genially. 'Why didn't you come to Tottenham?'

'I think I will next time,' said Greaves.

That next time had already started. Milan were lining up a Brazilian forward as Greaves's replacement, and Chelsea were rolling up their sleeves to haul him back. No chance. Tottenham was where Greaves wanted to be. To his mind, going back to Chelsea would be a backward step.

It was the same club that he had left – too many inexperienced players, a mid-table finish at best. Plus he really fancied playing for Spurs. They had made themselves the greatest team in the history of English football.

The £99,999 Tottenham paid for Greaves was always talked of as Nicholson's way of preventing his being saddled with the label of 'First £100,000 Player' but, according to Greaves, that was all wrong.

'It didn't make a blind bit of difference to me,' he revealed later in an interview in *The Tottenham Hotspur Opus*. 'Most people seemed to be under the impression that it was done for my benefit – to ease the pressure – but it wasn't. The deal could have been for ten million quid for all I cared. All I wanted to do was move to Tottenham Hotspur. I think Bill didn't want to be the first manager to pay that amount of money for a player, but it never made a scrap of difference to me – I didn't get any of the fee anyway! So contrary to it being done to take the pressure off, I really couldn't have cared less. I think Bill in his heart of hearts didn't want to be saddled with that £100,000 tag.'

The big question was who was going to be Greaves's strike partner: Smith or Allen? One of them had to lose out. They had both been off form, according to the *Daily Telegraph* of 9 December 1961, which reported Nicholson being: 'troubled by the failure of faithful servants to find their true form... A few weeks ago he dropped Les Allen and Bobby Smith, last season's marksmen. After a spell they returned and against West Bromwich last week Allen switched to centre-forward and Smith to inside-left. Allen scored, Smith did not, so for this afternoon's home game against Birmingham, Mackay takes over from Smith. Presumably this is only a temporary measure until Greaves is allowed to play League football. Mr Nicholson will then have the tricky problem of finding a place for both Smith and Mackay, two of the stalwarts of Spurs' "Double" team.'

Allen is always talked of as the one being dumped for Greaves, straight off, game over. When Nicholson spoke about it in his autobiography, he set the myth in stone. 'One of the saddest things was that I had to replace [Allen]... when Jimmy Greaves became available. I felt sorry for him. He had done nothing to deserve being replaced, but a football manager cannot afford sentiment.' Everyone went along with the myth, but Nicholson's memory was unreliable. It wasn't Allen who missed out initially; it was Smith who found himself out of the front line at first, with Allen taking over the number 9 shirt. Rewind to December 1961 and Greaves's debut against Blackpool at White Hart Lane. Greaves's hat-trick was all anyone wanted to talk about but, in between the Jimmy Greaves Show, Allen made it 3-0 in the first half and bagged another in the second. 'This partnership may become as famous as Derby County's great double act of Carter and Doherty,' was the *Daily Telegraph*'s prediction. 'Certainly the first appearance of Greaves in a Spurs shirt had a tremendous effect on Allen, who looked twice the player of a few weeks ago as he fought with tremendous determination to make sure of staying in the team.'

Smith, though, returned to the front line after a few weeks, and for the next two seasons the pair were in competition to play alongside Greaves. Smith had something that saw him favoured over Allen when it came to the big games: confidence, self-belief and a relish for the rough stuff. In the autobiographical *This One's On Me*, Greaves reminisced about the days when forwards were allowed to make physical contact with goalkeepers:

'I think Bobby would feel redundant in a match if he was playing in the modern game... [he] liked to let everybody know who was boss right from the word go... Because of his huge physical presence [he] tended to get labelled as a clumsy player. But he had a load of finesse and was exceptionally skilled at laying the ball off. He and I struck up a terrific partnership for England and Spurs and he was never given the full credit he deserved for helping my goal haul.'

It was Smith who partnered Greaves in the European Cup run, an enduring staple of Tottenham folklore: losing to Eusébio's Benfica over two legs in which Greaves had three goals disallowed for offside and claimed, 'We were refereed out of it.' It was Smith and Greaves who led the line in the 1962 FA Cup Final against Burnley. In the dressing room beforehand, Greaves had predicted he would score in the fourth minute – in fact only three minutes were up when Smith flicked the ball on for him to make it 1-0. Burnley equalised soon into the second half but Smith put Spurs back into the lead with one of his trademark swipes, swivelling and in the same movement lashing the ball home. It was 3-1 at the end thanks to Blanchflower's penalty goal.

That trophy had to be consolation for losing out on the title; Spurs were pipped close to the end of the season by Ipswich Town and Burnley. So there was no Double Double, let alone the Treble; no one achieved that type of glory back then, not even Jimmy Greaves. Retaining the FA Cup meant they were back in Europe, though – this time in the European Cup Winners' Cup, when Tottenham became the first English club to win a European trophy. Along the way came another classic Smith moment. As the team left the pitch after losing a first-leg tie against Bratislava, Smith clenched a fist at the centre-half who had been trying to rough him up all the way through. 'He said in a heavy Yorkshire accent: "Londres… Londres… You'll get yours in Lon-dres,"' recalled Greaves. 'The goalkeeper literally turned white. He knew what was coming. Smithy charged the goalkeeper into the back of the net in the first minute.'

The final against Atlético Madrid was in Rotterdam. Greaves scored the first with a half-volley from Smith's cross, and John White made it 2-0 with a fizzing left-footer. Atleti got one back, but then Dyson lobbed in Tottenham's third before providing the assist for Greaves to make it 4-1, and in the final moments the diminutive winger made a 40-yard run, looked up, found he had no one to pass to so just hammered home a shot by himself.

Which made it Dyson's night, really. Greaves liked to tell the story of how they were all sitting in the dressing room afterwards, having a fag, 'And Bobby says, "Here, Dyson, I'd retire now if I was you. You won't play like that again."' Witty himself, Greaves liked Smith's humour. In *This One's On Me*, which centred on his recovery from alcoholism, he spoke affectionately of his former strike partner, who roomed with him on both Tottenham and England duty and who 'sadly for him had a gambling sickness that became as difficult to control as my drinking problem':

'Bobby and I were good pals... even though he stretched our friendship to the limit with money requests to help him pay off gambling debts. [He] had the betting bug so bad that even when he was abroad with the Tottenham and England team he would still indulge himself. I would be lying on the bed in our room having an afternoon nap when suddenly I would hear Smithy shouting down the phone to a bookie in London... Then he would phone back and get the results. He was the most generous bloke walking this earth when he was a winner but unfortunately his losses were greater than his successes.'

In summer 1964, in hock to various turf accountants, Smith accepted the Fleet Street shilling as a means of paying them off. The club took offence at the comments published in his name and got rid of him to Division Four Brighton for an insulting £5,000.

Nicholson, of course, had Jimmy Greaves's new partner lined up already.

Postscript

Les Allen hung on longer than Bobby Smith, scoring his last league goal in late March 1965 in the 7-4 defenestration of Wolves at White Hart Lane, where his goal against Sheffield Wednesday had sealed the title in 1961. In the summer of 1965, he moved to Queens Park Rangers, where he scored 55 goals and was part of the side that won the League Cup in 1967.

'I had to speak to him a few times on behalf of the Tottenham Tribute Trust, which I'm proud to be a trustee of,' says Daniel Wynne. 'He was one of our first beneficiaries – the Trust funded his knee replacement. I phoned to see how he was getting on, and he was almost embarrassed. I think he was from that generation – a proud man. It was pretty much forced on him because he didn't want to be seen reaching out for help. He was stoical and dour. He came to work, did his job to the best of his ability, did it very well and then went home again. He didn't want the problems that come with fame, he didn't want the glory, he just did what he did and did it effectively.'

Some players, like Allen, are just destined to play the unsung hero.

Another Postscript

Danny Blanchflower was my childhood hero, but Bobby Smith, with his dark rumpled hair and wicked grin, was my teenage crush. Years later, when Rob White and I were writing *The Ghost of White Hart Lane*, I got to meet him. He tried to snog me, the sweet old thing.

We've Got the G-Men

Greaves and Gilzean

White Hart Lane, 20 August 1966

It's the first day of the 1966/67 season, a season that has to end in something big for the G-Men. Look at the league tables since they've been together: 1964/65, Manchester United and Leeds at the top, Tottenham sixth; 1965/66, Liverpool and Leeds at the top, Tottenham eighth. The G-Men are the best goal merchants in the league, they've been scoring for fun, but they have nothing to show for it.

It's almost a new side today. Up front is the template, the strike partnership feared by every defender: Jimmy Greaves plus one other. Once it was the chunky Smith bodying defenders out of the way; now it's Alan Gilzean, the lean and balding Scot whose main weapon of destruction is his head. Elsewhere on the field, Dave Mackay seems like the improbable survivor of a shipwreck, the one who's come back after a twice-broken leg, the only one left of the dazzlingly gifted midfield of 1962/63 who brought a European trophy to England for the first time. Blanchflower was already a middle-aged man when he finally left the stage at the end of the 1964/65 season; White had already gone, far, far too soon. The rebuilding has been underway since then; new players have come in – Pat Jennings, Cyril Knowles, Joe Kinnear and Terry Venables. Mike England, the tall, authoritative centre-back is making his debut. It's a big ask for him, having to show he's worth the £95,000 Nicholson splashed out on him. The ink is barely dry on his contract; just 24 hours back he was still a Blackburn Rover.

But while this might be shaping up to be the best side Bill Nicholson has produced for ages, they're pitted against one of Don Revie's dirtiest. It's been a nervy first half, the minutes rolling by like hours under a merciless August sun. A Johnny Giles header has put the away side in the lead with only 13 minutes gone, the lowest point in nearly three-quarters of an hour of Leeds hard-bastardry that includes a Billy Bremner special on

Dave Mackay. Oof, that's caught him on his newly healed leg. Mackay, temper ignited, chin jutting, grabs Bremner's collar and it looks for a moment as if he's going to lift his fellow Scot like a caber and hurl him out of the ground. No prizes for guessing which photo is going to illustrate this match on tomorrow's sports pages. It's an image that will go on to annoy Mackay for the rest of his days, portraying him as a thug. 'If he'd kicked the other one I could have accepted that,' he says later.

The incident seems to galvanise Spurs. Cliff Jones and Jimmy Robertson are running hard along the wings, and Gilzean is planted among the Leeds defence, causing all sorts of trouble with glancing headers. Venables is beginning to pick out Greaves with that intelligent passing of his, though it's actually Alan Mullery who flicks the switch, equalising with an outrageous 30-yarder. Now Spurs are back in the game, at full pelt. Seconds after the interval, Gilzean heads them in front. Leeds rally, but England and Jennings deal with it. Then comes the final flourish: a cheeky 20-yarder from Greaves to make it 3-1. And around the ground, the chorus rises up from the terraces:

We've got the G-Men, Greaves and Gilzean
They're the world's greatest scoring machine

Long before Glenn Hoddle ascended to the throne, it was Alan Gilzean who was celebrated in terrace song as the King of White Hart Lane. The fans had their first sight of Greaves's next strike partner in a game that no one would have wished for but had to happen. Every Spurs fan alive and sentient in July 1964 can remember where they were and what they were doing when they heard John White was dead, killed by a freak accident: a lightning strike in a thunderstorm over Crews Hill golf course. The John White Memorial Match, Spurs v a Scotland XI, was to raise funds for White's 22-year-old widow Sandra, left to raise a toddler and five-month-old baby on her own.

The Spurs XI included White's younger brother Tom, the Aberdeen striker who dreamed of a permanent place at Tottenham Hotspur. He scored that day, from a Jimmy Greaves pass, but it was his fellow Scot, Gilzean, whose nine goals had taken Dundee to a European Cup semi-final and on whom Nicholson had his sights set.

Bill Nicholson's word for the Scot's playing style was 'unorthodox, different in many ways from Bobby Smith'. You could say that again. No other striker of that era was like Gilzean, who could jump and seemingly hang in the air, who moved around the penalty area as though following the angles of a threepenny bit. No other *footballer* was like him, come to that. In his autobiography, *Glory Glory: My Life with Spurs*, Nicholson wrote: 'He was more of a footballing centre-forward and started his career as an inside-left. He didn't head the ball full on like Smith. He preferred to glance it as he turned his head. It was not a style you could coach in anyone because the margin of error was so small. But it suited him and I never tried to change him.' Miljan Miljanić, manager of Red Star Belgrade, once said: 'If ever a football university is founded, Alan Gilzean should be appointed as the first professor to lecture on how to use one's head and to play with one's head.'

It was a style that you could, well, find it difficult to get your head round at first. 'I never got Gilzean when I was a youngster,' says Ivan Cohen. 'As a footballer he was too sophisticated – he was very subtle in his play. It was only when I watched videos of him later, with a more trained eye than when I was young, that I suddenly got it. He made the players around him. He was the catalyst.'

You get the impression, too, that he was Nicholson's perfect player, the kind of man he liked just as a man: 'He was easy to talk to, never moaned and got on with the job in an uncomplicated way. I could be open and frank with him and he wouldn't get angry or sulk. He was very trustworthy and likeable. Away from football he was something of a loner, a quiet, unaggressive man. I never had any problem with Gilly and, unlike some of today's footballers, he wasn't greedy when it came to money.'

Nicholson wasn't alone in his appreciation; everyone liked Gilzean. 'We hit it off on and off the pitch,' said Greaves. 'He was great, possibly the best footballer I've ever played with, a blood brother. He was a character, but he could really play and he had the most wonderful footballing brain. I had a bit of that sort of telepathy with Bobby Smith, but Gilly and I played together a lot longer.' Not that it took long for them to establish the partnership. The most G-Men thing ever is that Greaves once passed up an open-goal opportunity because he was too busy chatting to his strike partner.

'It was a relationship,' said Alan Mullery. 'As soon as they went on the field they reacted in the way you would if you'd been living with your wife for 50 years. You know exactly what she's going to do. It was like that with Jimmy and Gilly. They were the two best forwards in the country. You had people like Denis Law and George Best playing in those days but as a pair Greaves and Gilzean were fantastic.'

Steve Perryman was there when Jimmy and Gilly met up late in their lives, and the experience has stayed with him. 'To see those two greats look at each other and smile and laugh at what the other one was saying – the mutual respect was just oozing out of them.' By that time, of course, a lot of commentators were making comparisons between Gilzean and Dimitar Berbatov, but in a way you could never liken Gilly to any other player because there was much more to him than what he achieved in play. The best summing-up I've read of the enigma that was Alan Gilzean is by Hunter

Davies, who came across him in the early 1970s while working on his fly-on-the-dressing-room-wall masterpiece *The Glory Game*. This is what he wrote more than 25 years later in the *New Statesman*: 'I can remember that his wife was a policewoman, that he liked a drink and was dead lazy – getting into his Jag to drive a hundred yards to the newsagent. But what I mainly recall is something I have never come across in a footballer before – he had little interest in football. It was just a job.'

Tales of his capacity for alcohol abound. He was a fully paid-up member of the drinking school in the back room of the Bell and Hare where, according to Greaves, he 'would sit up at the bar like a king on his throne and would invariably get the first order. He was the only one who could keep pace with Dave Mackay.' There was the time a supporter complained to Nicholson that he'd spotted Gilzean coming out of a nightclub at two o'clock in the morning, to which the Spurs players pointed out that, on the contrary, he was actually going *into* the club. On another occasion the team were playing a pre-season tournament in Amsterdam, where a military tattoo was taking place simultaneously, and the players were sitting at a table outside a bar. A Scottish regiment came marching past and, on recognising Gilzean, hailed him warmly. Gilzean left the table to talk to them and was last seen marching back to barracks with them, the sergeant's sash draped over his shoulder. It was 24 hours before the team saw him again.

'If I went *slightly* off the rails it would be led by Gilly,' says Steve Perryman, who made his first-team debut as an 18-year-old in 1969:

'He had this love of Greek restaurants. I went probably three or four times with him to one round the corner from Tottenham Court Road, and Gilly had his own bottles there. They were marked – he was a pro in everything he did! Every single thing, he did it right. He would put everything into perspective for me. Bill Nicholson was the man who talked football. Gilly could add a bit of life *within* the football, the sort of situations that you wouldn't ever get into with your manager. But he was a top line player, so how Bill ever roomed me with Gilly – well, I cannot quite see it. But I think that tells you a lot about Bill's attitude towards him. "Gilly might lead you slightly off the way, but it'll be the right way, whatever it is." He was definitely like a teacher to me. What a man, what a man.'

It wasn't even as though Gilzean looked the part. In the wonderful *In Search of Alan Gilzean*, the author James Morgan described him as looking like 'someone's elderly father'. 'He looked more like a civil servant than a footballer, tall and clerical in a dark suit,' wrote John Moynihan in that lovely book, *The Soccer Syndrome*. 'It doesn't seem possible that he was one of the finest passers of the ball in football. Centre-forwards like Tommy Lawton or Dixie Dean stood out – rough, bullet-headed, occasionally flexing their neck muscles. Gilzean stood there shyly as if he had just arrived on honeymoon.'

You get the picture. To see Alan Gilzean for what he was – one of the greatest players of his, or any, generation – required imagination. He was a kind of human miracle, someone who took in spectacular amounts of booze without its having any effect on his game. 'The strolling, the swagger, the drinking,' recalls Perryman. 'I don't think it cost him anything in his game. It just added to his character and his way.'

In his laid-back way, too, he was brave, a stoic. 'Inevitably such a performer received copious punishment from desperate opponents,' wrote Ivan Ponting in *Tottenham Hotspur: Player by Player*, 'but he was not lacking in heart and accepted the blows as part of his job, preferring to retaliate with skill rather than violence.' Perryman concurs: 'I remember Frank Lampard Snr laying one on him. Gilly just took it. He didn't even look back at Lampard. His attitude was just, "There you go. That's not right. But no big deal, no fuss. That's how life is."'

That 1966/67 season was like a lot of others that Spurs fans have experienced. Greaves scored 25 in 38 games in the league, and six in eight games in the FA Cup. Gilzean's numbers were 12 in the league and three in the Cup. It was a scoring performance that should have brought Spurs the title, but in the end they were a nearly side again, third behind Manchester United and Nottingham Forest. The G-Men got their silverware, though. The semi-final against Forest at Hillsborough was no cruise; they went 2-0 up through Greaves and the reserve-team player Frank Saul but had to hang on after Forest came up with a late goal. In the final at Wembley, Chelsea's Ron Harris stuck so close to Greaves they might as well have been welded, and Gilzean didn't get on the scoresheet either, but he led the forward line brilliantly, setting up the conditions in the first half for Jimmy Robertson to drive home a ball that had bounced off Harris's shins. After the restart Robertson touched on a long throw-in from Mackay, and Saul's thunderball of a shot made it 2-0. Bobby Tambling pulled one back for Chelsea, but it was too late to make any difference.

As a teenager Saul had looked the part of the star Spurs striker in the making. He was strong, keen and skilful, and during the Double season he was Bobby Smith's deputy at centre-forward. Here was a player who could go all the way, you thought, an England youth international who, in 1962, found the net twice against Feyenoord during Tottenham's European Cup run. In 1964, expected to take over after Bobby Smith left for Brighton, he had an extended spell as Greaves's strike partner and scored five in the first four games, including a hat-trick at home to Burnley. And then Gilzean turned up and Saul was back in the shadows. He didn't give up. Determined to show his worth, he started playing out wide, was stand-in at centre-forward again and had 20 outings in each of his last four seasons. Having scored against Forest in the Cup semi, Saul had now scored the goal that clinched the 1967 FA Cup.

He can't have imagined what was coming up next.

Chivers Scores, Park Lane Roars

Chivers and Gilzean

January 1968, a night game at Hillsborough. Flashlights are detonating around the pitch where the snappers are crowded to record every movement of the most expensive footballer in Britain. The 22-year-old Martin Chivers is Tottenham's latest signing and he's something else again to look at, a scowling lion of a youth with a mane of blond curls, massive shoulders (just think of those throw-ins) and plenty of time to contemplate his future because all the action is up the other end.

So far all it's been is attack, attack, attack, and when Wednesday finally get past Jennings's defences in the 42nd minute the only surprise is that it took them so long, because the last time

Spurs won away to Sheffield Wednesday Hitler was marching into Austria. Except this time it's different and it only takes a couple of minutes for everything to change because Chivers is suddenly chasing after a loose ball. He crosses in low, Gilzean sweeps a shot towards the far post and Greaves nips in for the equaliser. And the second half is going the same way as the first, with Wednesday doing all the pressing, right up until three minutes from the final whistle, when the golden boy picks up another loose ball just inside his own half and runs with it till he sees the opening and hits the 20-yard winner past Ron Springett. £125,000 plus Frank Saul – it's money well spent.

Saul had been a Cup hero for all of six weeks when Nicholson called him into his office, which every Spurs player knew was never a good sign. He was told that Southampton had made an offer for him, and he, Nicholson, had his eye on a young lad there, and that was that. As Saul left for the south coast, makeweight in the deal that brought Chivers to Tottenham Hotspur, a barrage of questions rose up: was this a new formation, Chivers as third wheel behind Greaves and Gilzean? Or was this the end of the G-Men? And, if so, which one would get the elbow? The only certainty was that Spurs had a new scoring machine. A week and a half later Chivers bagged both goals in Tottenham's 2-2 draw against Manchester United at Old Trafford in the third round of the FA Cup. Again, money well spent. Then, ten weeks into the 1968/69 season, something bad happened to him.

The problem had started in pre-season. Every time Chivers put his left foot down to drive the ball with his right, it hurt. That July, the club sent him to a specialist but the cortisone injections didn't work – he had knee pain all through August. Towards the end of September, with Spurs at home to Nottingham Forest, he went to lay the ball off with his right foot and just collapsed. There was a big hole where his knee should have been and his kneecap was at the top of his thigh. John Pratt took one look at it and was nearly sick. Chivers was out for nigh on a year and the club were calling their insurers because they thought he was finished, his career derailed at 23. Small wonder that he was an awkward sod when he came back.

In an echo of Hunter Davies's summing-up of Alan Gilzean, these are the main things that come to mind when I think about Martin Chivers: his two front teeth had to be replaced by a denture, not because they had been dislodged on the field of battle, he disclosed, but because bad teeth ran in his family; his mother was German and he had a German O Level; he drove Bill Nicholson mad.

The injury must have affected him badly, but Nicholson just thought he was lazy and timid. Nicholson would think nostalgically of Bobby Smith coming into the dressing room after a match, with ballooned ankles and knees the colour of red cabbage but not uttering a single whimper. Chivers had this marvellous physical presence – why didn't he use those magnificent shoulders to his advantage, why was he so unaggressive, why had he no fight in him?

As for Chivers, he found the stick he was getting so bad he would sometimes leave the dressing room to get away from it. Nicholson and his assistant Eddie Baily thought he was slow. Far from it; he was just one of those players who made it look easy because he was so good. That was the problem – sometimes he didn't look as if he was trying.

'He was probably the only player I found it almost impossible to get along with because of his moods,' Nicholson reflected later. 'He was the sort who drains the enthusiasm out of a manager.' 'The arguments I used to get in with Bill over him,' said Alan Mullery. 'He used to think Martin was lazy. I didn't care how lazy he was as long as he won us football matches. He was a fantastic goalscorer.'

* * *

Opinions differ as to when Greaves's alcohol consumption stopped being a convivial release from the stress of playing and instead became self-destructive and problematic. Nicholson had thought for a while that he was in decline, not the player he had been. Reflexes, he said, were the first thing to go with a footballer, and Greaves's game was all about lightning reactions. That said, contrary to Nicholson's judgement, Greaves went on being a goal hound all the way through the 1968/69 season; his 32 in the league included two hat-tricks and a four, as well as one of his finest goals ever. Spurs were at home to Leicester City when, wide on the halfway line, he met Pat Jennings's clearance, shrugged off his marker, dribbled past three more defenders and dummied Peter Shilton before slipping the ball into the net.

The season that followed was where it stopped. The goals didn't dry up but he seemed to have a dwindling supply, one in every three games whereas in the past it would be one in every two and the occasional multiple. Thing was, his game was all about goals, he wasn't there for anything else, so when Spurs drew 0-0 at home to Crystal Palace in the fourth round of the FA Cup and then days later lost by one goal in the replay, Nicholson brought out the scythe. Five first-teamers were dropped for the league game against Southampton three days later. The bodies included not just Greaves but Gilzean. Gilzean came back in after a few games but Greaves didn't.

Greaves knew he had lost his appetite for the game. A spell in the reserves would do him good. He spoke to Nicholson about it, and was under the impression his manager had given the okay. Instead, the ruthlessness with which Nicholson had dispatched Bobby Smith was now turned on his one-time striking partner.

'A little while later I was home when Bill called,' Greaves recalled years later in an interview in *The Tottenham Hotspur Opus*. 'He told me he had Martin Peters in his office. I thought, *Right, okay*. I didn't give it a second thought until he told me that he wanted me to leave Spurs and that my time was finished at White Hart Lane.'

Greaves felt as if all his breath had been taken away. Shaken, he asked Nicholson if he was sure, but was told that it would be better for the club if he left. Then Nicholson added that Ron Greenwood was waiting to speak to him with regard to his joining West Ham. 'To be honest, it was the death knell for me,' he said later. 'I was really taken aback by it. I didn't want to leave Spurs, I really didn't. But then, what could I do? Martin Peters was in Bill's office. It all seemed pretty final. I just got the feeling he didn't want me there any more. That was it. My life at Spurs was over.'

It was the end of the G-Men. The saddest thing about it was the way Greaves left, or rather it was the way they left him. The day after Bill's call, he went to the club to pick up his things and get his boots, and no one was there.

'Bill had made sure that everyone was down at Cheshunt, at the training ground. There wasn't a soul in the ground.

'It was like clearing out your desk at work when you leave. I couldn't say goodbye to anybody, because there wasn't anybody there. And I knew that he had done it on purpose because it happened on a Friday and the team never went to Cheshunt on a Friday.'

Looking back at it some 40 years on, though, Greaves could only talk with love about the club he'd chosen to grace with his enchanting gifts. 'I wasn't disappointed we didn't win a title,' he said. 'I loved playing at Spurs. It was the summertime of my career, and I would have played there for ever if I could.'

Words like these make you wish that by some miracle there could be no such thing as mortality any more, that you could reverse the process of ageing, that somehow Jimmy Greaves could still be around, for ever like he says, so light and lovely as he darts towards goal, the magician, the genius, Messi before Messi ever existed, the spiky-haired boy in baggy shorts.

* * *

Maybe he just needed Greaves to go, but for the next four years Chivers was outstanding, the best centre-forward in Europe. With Martin Peters now in the squad, Nicholson was able to tweak the playing style a bit and the new Chivers–Gilzean strike partnership established another golden era for Spurs. Far from being a burden, the responsibilities of being the main goalscorer seemed to galvanise Chivers. His two goals in the 1971 League Cup Final against Aston Villa won it for Spurs; his trademark 25-yarder and soaring header against Wolves at Molineux in the first leg of the 1972 UEFA Cup Final gave Spurs the foundations of their victory in the return leg.

The 1973 League Cup Final against Norwich City wasn't the greatest. After 72 minutes of deadlock Chivers launched a long throw into the box where Duncan Forbes, the defender, could only deflect the ball in Gilzean's direction. Gilzean angled a header back to Mike England, who couldn't get to it, but Ralph Coates came skittering in to follow up with a low, slammed shot that went in off the far post.

It was the only goal of the game, and the first ever one scored by a substitute at Wembley, so all the attention was centred on that. But it was those massive shoulders of Martin Chivers that made it happen.

Crooks and Archie Up Front for Spurs

Archibald and Crooks

Selhurst Park, 19 August 1980

The game was only eight minutes old when Garth Crooks powered in a perfect header from Hoddle's corner kick. Then, at the speed of cat burglars spotting an open window, he and Steve Archibald played a one-two between Crystal Palace's flimsy defence for Crooks to slip in and score again. Only 19 minutes gone and Spurs were running away with it already. Well, not quite, not on a day when they had to rely on their third-choice keeper, Mark Kendall; he was beaten soon after by Vince Hilaire from a ridiculous angle. But then Hoddle made it 3-1, with a fierce right-foot shot that Archibald's pass had made possible.

This was Spurs, so obviously they weren't going to make it easy on themselves. Palace hauled back the deficit to make it 3-2, a poor back-pass from the usually immaculate Chris Hughton letting in Neil Smillie, Kendall late to see it coming. Palace, though, seemed equally inclined to do things the hard way. Outraged by advantage being played rather than a free kick given when he was fouled by Paul Miller, Hilaire bowled the referee off his feet with a two-handed shove. Red card incoming. Palace lost concentration as well as their key man and Archibald immediately restored Tottenham's two-goal lead. It still wasn't over – Jim Cannon floated Palace's third over Kendall from a long way out – but it wasn't enough to deny Spurs both points.

Crystal Palace 3 Tottenham Hotspur 4. Never mind the leaky defence. The fans had waited and waited for this, a strike partnership that actually worked: Steve Archibald and Garth Crooks, the sharers of the biggest, huggiest goal celebrations, the transformative pairing that took Tottenham back to the place they hadn't been since 1972. The place called glory.

Let's recap. Gilzean left the building in the summer of 1974, taking all of that class and subtlety with him. Just after the start of the following season, Bill Nicholson – architect of four of the greatest strike partnerships in Spurs history but now despairing of ever getting it right again – had thrown down his cards. Terry Neill took over, but rapidly hightailed it back to Arsenal, his spiritual home, leaving his coach, Keith Burkinshaw, to oversee the forthcoming collapse.

Attempts to find a new strike partnership hadn't paid off. Chris Jones was a lovely mover but became known as the nearly man because he usually *nearly* scored. John Duncan, reliable and competent, hadn't clicked with Chivers either and anyway, by the time Burkinshaw took over, Chivers had left to play for Servette in Switzerland. Peter Taylor could knock them in but he was a winger. Gerry Armstrong was fun, a great character and a hard worker, but more of an individual finisher. Not quite the Spurs style.

Ian Moores, in contrast, should have been right up Tottenham's street. He'd arrived in August 1976 from Stoke City and was hailed as an England centre-forward in the making, a 21-year-old with defence-skittling power in the air, already two Under-23 caps for England, a hairdo that was half Günter Netzer and half Britt Ekland, and the cachet of a lot of big clubs being after him. White Hart Lane was meant to be the ideal career destination for him, and he had made a cracking start to it – on the scoresheet in the League Cup opener against Middlesbrough, and banging one in on his league debut in Spurs' 3-2 win against Manchester United at Old Trafford at the start of that September. After that, not a lot. North London was where he flatlined. The whole team did. From being the great Cup side of the early 1970s, Spurs turned into the one that seeped goals all the way through the 1976/77 season, leaking five against Manchester City at the bitter end to put them rock bottom of the table and send them down.

That season in the Second Division has passed into folklore, mind. Getting back into the top tier came down to goal difference in the end, and it was largely due to one single match and a strike partnership so short-lived it was more like a blind date. Spurs v Bristol Rovers on 27 October 1977 was the one that gave them the numbers, a record-smashing win achieved with a makeshift front line because of injuries, with the aforementioned striker whose name the fans were already rhyming with Never Scores, and another who had only signed on the dotted line 48 hours back. The Leo Sayer-haired Colin Lee had joined from Torquay that Thursday, had been thrown straight in on the Saturday because so many of the senior squad were injured, and scored four. Ian Moores got a hat-trick.

Tottenham Hotspur 9 Bristol Rovers 0. Out there on the pitch, the fans were swarming the moment the final whistle went, teenage boys in jeans and 1970s jerseys jumping over barriers, waving their arms. This was champagne after stale beer, a shower of coins from the fruit machine. This was Glenn Hoddle still a few days short of his 20th birthday, already powerful in his boots, coming up with those passes no other player in England could make. This was an unsung hero, Peter Taylor, taking corners bang on the mark, every single time, and Barry Daines practically twiddling his thumbs in goal because all the action was up the other end. For a long time afterwards, the Bristol Rovers keeper's dreams would have featured re-runs of fishing the ball out of his own net, including four in the last ten minutes. There were so many goals that the *Daily Telegraph*'s reporter inadvertently left one out and had to add it on the end, like a PS: 'Spurs' other goal came from Taylor just before half-time.'

Bolton went on to be promoted as champions, while Spurs and Southampton followed them up thanks to a last-day-of-the-season 0-0 draw which suited them both. Next came the boldest deal of the decade, maybe even the century. Ossie Ardiles and Ricky Villa, two World Cup winners, were signed in 1978 by a club that had just been promoted back to the First Division. Now they had the best midfield in England. Now all they needed was an effective strike partnership.

'Ossie and Ricky coming to us was our "promotion" to the next level, if you like to call it that,' says Steve Perryman. 'Two World Cup winners gave us built-in status. They made our team decent enough for Archie and Garth to join us, thinking *I'm joining a club that might win something.* It sounds disrespectful to the ones that were there before Archie and Garth, but actually those players weren't at that level. They didn't have the pace. None of them had the sort of cutting-edge class that Archie and Garth had. Break through, one v one, goal! They both wanted to score. That sounds a stupid thing to say – why would you be on the pitch if you didn't want to score? – but I think they *expected* to score, and if one couldn't score they wanted the other one to score. They were a partnership that fought for each other.

'I think I played a part in Garth coming to us, as it happens. Ray Evans, who signed pro for Tottenham the same year as me, later went on to play for Stoke, where Garth had come up through the youth team. So Garth had let it be known that he was looking for a move and Ray phoned me: "Do you think your manager might be interested?" I didn't know, but I put it to Keith, and that started the process. It doesn't mean anything comes of that sort of conversation every time, but it was the Tottenham link between Ray and me that helped Garth get to us. I think Garth was very interested in getting to London anyway because he was already doing a bit of DJ-ing and that was obviously easier to do in London than anywhere else. I'm not saying it dominated his thinking, but it was in his mind that if he was going to London he might just get involved in Capital Radio and all that sort of stuff.'

The Glasgow-born Archibald, meanwhile, had only been a professional footballer for two years, but he had packed a lot into that time. Having started his career in midfield with Clyde, while running a business looking after high-end motors on the side, he was signed by Alex Ferguson's Aberdeen, becoming part of the team that won the Scottish title. Crooks, it followed, regarded him as the senior partner.

As personalities, they were very different. Crooks was a witty extravert who, once in London, got his radio career going as a sideline. Archibald was taciturn, most definitely his own man. He had been in the real world, running his own business. It lent him maturity; the juvenile banter of the dressing room didn't sit well with him. Theo Delaney recalls Glenn Hoddle reminiscing about him while backstage on *The Spurs Show*: 'Yeah, we all went out together – except Steve, of course. We never had a problem with him, he just never hung out with us. He did his own thing.'

'Terry Venables once told me why he'd signed Archie at Barcelona,' recalls Perryman. 'He said it was because Archie was a loner, so he wouldn't have any problems about being on his own in a new country.'

'They couldn't have been more different,' says Theo Delaney. 'Black players were beginning to break through by the end of the 1970s but they were still getting unbelievable stick. In 1980 the National Front were very openly selling their magazine, *The Bulldog*, outside the ground. They were a force – the far right rearing its ugly head. On the way in you'd have the National Front and once you'd got in you'd have Crooks and Archibald. To have that partnership right at the top of our team, a black guy and a white guy in harmony – it was the Stevie Wonder and Paul McCartney collaboration "Ebony and Ivory" embodied by Archibald and Crooks.'

That harmony had been there right from the start. They had come across each other before, on opposite sides at Under-21 internationals, so they knew each other could play, and quickly made themselves into a unit. Early on, it was Us against Them. They were reunited on *The Spurs Show*, interviewed by Theo Delaney and Mike Leigh, a couple of years ago and they spoke of their early weeks with Tottenham. At one stage Crooks found himself thinking, *This is going to end badly.*

'We had a difficult few pre-season training sessions and games,' recalled Crooks. 'We sort of tried to get an understanding and at the time I thought, *We're hardly getting a touch of the ball here.* The whole thing was being dominated by midfield. Ardiles and Hoddle were passing the ball wherever they wanted because they were so good they could do that. It would go from Hoddle to Ardiles, from Ardiles back to someone else, and we'd look at each other and think, *We might get a chance here* – and that went on for about four or five games. We weren't getting any service. It got to a stage where people were saying, "They're not scoring goals," and Archie was getting angry. I said, "Don't worry, I just want to try something. Stay right up as far as you can on the back man and the next time the ball comes from Glenn or Ossie I'm not going to play it back to them, I'm just going to put it round the corner for you, I'm going to turn and we'll play it from there." We played a one-two and he was in on goal. Then it happened a second time. Glenn turned to Burkinshaw and said, "What's going on?" And Burkinshaw, to his credit, said, "Let them play on. Keep it going." And that was the beginning of the partnership.'

'We knew what we had to do,' concurred Archibald. 'We had to score goals for the club to be a success. You can have the best midfield player in the world but he isn't going to score all the goals. A midfield player doesn't dictate to me as a striker to make a run – I dictate to the midfield player.'

'Nobody pushed Archie around,' says Delaney. 'I remember one interviewer asking him what it was like to play under Alex Ferguson. Did he realise he was in the presence of greatness? And Archie was like, "No I did not! I'm not that sort of guy! No one's going to make me impressed!"'

He definitely wasn't presenting Burkinshaw with flowers and chocolates either, as Crooks recalled: 'I remember Burkinshaw saying in the dressing room before one game, "Right, we're defending this corner. Crooksy, I want you here. And Archie, I want you back in the box, defending." And Archie went, "You what? No, I'm not doing that. I fucking score goals."'

They both did. Their flame burned brightest in that first season together, when their goals were a key part of Tottenham's return to the big time, Archibald scoring 25 in all competitions and Crooks 21. 'Crooks would find space with low gravity darts in between defenders,' says Toby Benjamin, co-author of *My Eyes Have Seen the Glory*. 'He was electrifying over short distances. Archibald's positioning in the box was uncanny. He often scored a poacher's goal but was no slouch and could hold off defenders with the ball. He had a terrific shot and scored quite a few from the edge of the area. It was his speciality, and seems to be rather forgotten about.'

That reminds me of something. The evening before Spurs played Wolves in the FA Cup semi-final at Hillsborough, Ivan Cohen was in the final year of his doctorate at Sheffield University and had rolled up with a group of Spurs-supporting friends at the hotel where Spurs were staying, hoping for autographs. 'Some of the team were in the bar,' recalls Ivan. 'There were about half a dozen of us, and Keith Burkinshaw pulled out a £20 note and bought us a round of drinks. £20 in those

84

days was a fortune! He was genial, not the dour Yorkshireman that you'd think, and somebody said to him, "Why does Archibald never score with his feet? He only gets headers." And Keith turned round and said, "I don't fucking care if he scores with his knob."'

Archibald did in fact score with his feet, a tap-in, the very next day. That was the ill-fated semi-final when, after Tottenham had led 2-1 till the dying minutes, Kenny Hibbitt's notorious dive won Wolves an equalising penalty. The victorious replay was at Highbury, where Spurs ran rampant and Crooks scored one of his best-loved goals, speeding to head home Hoddle's delicate lob. The Wembley final against Manchester City went to a replay too. Spurs were on the wrong end of a 2-1 scoreline when Archibald found space in the penalty area and Hoddle pushed the ball forward for him. It rolled off the end of his foot but Crooks stretched out to knock it home: 2-2, the golden equaliser, and a euphoric Crooks gazing up at the scoreboard and dreamily murmuring to Archibald, 'My name in lights.' We all know how it went after that – Ricky Villa's famous zigzag run through the

City defenders, everyone bawling at him to pass, and Crooks's air-kick as Villa finally released his shot to bring the FA Cup back to Tottenham.

Spurs went on to win a second successive FA Cup, and the UEFA Cup in 1984. Looking back, though, Archibald and Crooks never quite hit those levels of 1980/81 again. They made a belated start to the 1981/82 season due to injury, and in 1982/83 Archibald fell out big time with Burkinshaw and was dropped for a run of four games, though he still managed to clock up 21 goals. But slowly the partnership began to drift apart. Alan Brazil arrived from Ipswich Town in March 1983 and the following season a Crooks goal drought saw him going out on loan to Manchester United. The end came when Archibald left Tottenham for Barcelona.

'It's quite emotional thinking about that 81–84 squad,' says Toby Benjamin. 'I'll always love them.' He remembers how, early on, someone had painted ARCHIE AND CROOKS UP FRONT FOR SPURS on one of the gates, and it stayed there for ages long after they'd gone. The gate's gone now too, with the rest of the stadium, but in Benjamin's mind's eye it'll always be there. And it was going to be something of a wait before Tottenham had another strike partnership to go down in history. Not that that was down to any deficiency in personnel; it was just that, for one season, half a partnership was all they needed.

Clive's Fantastic Season

Clive Allen (with a little help from Hoddle and Waddle)

Villa Park, 23 August 1986

Aston Villa 0 Clive Allen 3. The new season was just four minutes old when Allen stroked home Tony Galvin's centre, and 23 minutes older when he hit the target from Glenn Hoddle's free kick, though he left the last part of his hat-trick – a 77th-minute tap-in from his cousin Paul – until the second half. Two days later he scored at home in the 1-1 draw against Newcastle United, and by mid-October if you added in what he'd done in the League Cup he was already on 14 goals, four more than he'd managed in the whole of the previous season.

Jimmy Greaves interviewed him on *Saint and Greavsie*: 'My record's there to be beaten,' he said of his 44 in a season in all competitions.

'You're well on the way.' 'No, it's impossible, just impossible,' Allen had responded. But people were saying it was a rebirth, a reviving of a career that had started so promisingly then gone awry in the weirdest possible way before getting worse.

Clive Allen was born a fortnight after his father, Les, had won the Double. He'd trained as a schoolboy with Spurs, done his apprenticeship with Queens Park Rangers and then in 1980 looked to be airlifted straight into the big time when Arsenal splashed out a million for him, a record back then for a teenager. Just 64 days later they swapped him for the Crystal Palace full-back Kenny Sansom, so he had a year at Selhurst Park before he went back to Loftus Road, like he'd strayed into the plot of *Groundhog Day*. 'It was a bizarre set of circumstances,' he said later, 'but I grew up in a very short time.'

His 40 goals in 87 appearances for Queens Park Rangers prompted an offer from Spurs in 1984. He was signed by Peter Shreeve, who had been assistant to Keith Burkinshaw there till the trophy-winning Yorkshireman walked out, at which point Shreeve was given an upgrade to manager. The plan was for Allen to replace Steve Archibald, but in his first season a bad injury forced him out of the game for a year. All big things for a lad to get through, and meanwhile he missed out on Tottenham's third-place finish that – combined with Shreeve bringing Chris Waddle down from Newcastle that summer – had left the fans' hopes sky-high, especially when the winger scored twice on his league debut in the 4-0 home rout of Watford. 'It can be boring on the wing if you're not getting the ball,' he said, so he went inside and fetched it.

A year later, and Spurs had failed to follow through. Tenth was the best they could do, and Shreeve was booted out. In his place came David Pleat, whose highest achievement up to that point had been to save Luton Town from the drop into the Second Division, a feat accomplished in the final game of the 1982/83 season after a late goal by Raddy Antić against Manchester City. The question that everyone was asking, it followed, was whether Pleat had the pedigree for a club with Tottenham's ambitions, which serves to illustrate how wrong they were, because it was Pleat's genius that brought about Clive Allen's golden year.

That 1986/87 season would turn out to be Pleat's only full one as Tottenham manager, but it featured some of the best attacking football of that era. You can remember it a lot of ways: the season they had Richard Gough; the one they went for the title but finished third; the one in which they lost the FA Cup to Coventry through a freak own goal by Gary Mabbutt. Or you can remember it as the season Allen broke the record.

It was some side. They had Ray Clemence in goal and a central defence that combined Gough with Gary Mabbutt, who was just reaching his peak. The midfield was poised to develop into something else again: Waddle out wide, Steve Hodge, Paul Allen, Ossie Ardiles and Hoddle, whom Pleat had absolved of all defensive responsibilities and so was free to let rip. In those early days, though, came a few sub-par results before everything started to happen, before Allen's goals began to come with machine-gun force – a penalty against Chelsea (they lost that one 3-1) and braces in consecutive weeks against Leicester City and Everton. After that came the breakthrough, the raising of everyone's hopes that this was going to be Tottenham's year.

It was the second week of October, at Anfield. Liverpool 0 Tottenham Hotspur 1, and this was Kenny Dalglish's Liverpool they'd done it to, the team of Ian Rush, Alan Hansen, Jan Mølby, Ronnie Whelan. 'It is hard to think of any side who have given Liverpool a lesson in passing on their own ground,' was the verdict of David Lacey in *The Guardian*. The early departure of the young striker Mark Falco to Watford had left Allen largely on his own up front, mind, and the day had featured the debut of what was assumed to be his new strike partner. Pleat had brought in Nico Claesen for £800,000 from Standard Liège, on the strength of a good World Cup as part of a Belgium side that finished fourth. The fans were excited. Allen and Claesen – this could be the new Archibald and Crooks. Like Crooks, Claesen had terrific pace and the plan was for him to do what Crooks did: hurtle on to those long, supernaturally precise balls from Hoddle. He scored his first goal for Spurs on 8 November, away to Norwich City. Okay, they lost, but otherwise it was all good. Then came the game against Oxford United.

These were days when pretty much every side in the land played either 4-4-2 or 4-2-4, and at

Tottenham Hotspur 4-4-2 was working well. But sometimes they'd try alternative shapes in training, and the day before they were due to travel to the Manor Ground they tried out 4-5-1. According to Glenn Hoddle, Pleat dropped the bombshell at the team meeting afterwards. 'This is how we're going to play tomorrow,' Pleat announced. 'If it doesn't work I'll take the blame, but it's going to work. Any objections?'

There were, as it happened. Ray Clemence gave it a resounding raspberry, pointing out that when he'd kept goal for Liverpool they'd tried it and met with minimal success. Hoddle wasn't that thrilled either, and nor were some of the others, and that day against Oxford they went 2-0 down after 20 minutes. Then Allen scored twice, Waddle added two more and after that it flowed.

It was the game that ended Claesen's Tottenham career, really. Allen didn't need the strike partner that the Belgian was brought in to be. Allen had Waddle to feed him from the wing, he had Hoddle's exquisite passes. Now part of the five-man midfield, Claesen was there more or less on sufferance, out of place. The 24-year-old was quick, he beavered away, but he was a striker rather than a multi-skilled forward. That being the case, he might as well not have bothered to turn up. This season was all about Clive Allen.

Looking at it now, it's all just numbers. You had to be there. In the League Cup fourth round it was 3-1 away to Cambridge United (two for him there), though his brace against Nottingham Forest in the league still had them on the wrong side of the scoresheet, as Forest got three. Spurs went up to Old Trafford at the end of the first week in December – it was one of the first Sunday games to be televised – and he scored again in the 3-3 draw, a diving header. Gordon Strachan kicked him and broke his nose. 'It was a fabulous game,' Allen said. By the end of the month, he seemed unstoppable – two every game, at Stamford Bridge, at White Hart Lane against West Ham, and at Highfield Road, though that was in a 3-4 defeat that would come back to bite them later on. At the start of February he scored his second hat-trick of the season, in the second leg of the League Cup fifth round – West Ham again, 5-0. The week after, in the semi-final first leg away to Arsenal, he won it for Spurs in extra time with the only goal of the game. It brought his tally to 34.

'Clive only ever played the width of the box,' said Waddle later. 'He never ran down the flanks and we basically passed teams off the park. Ossie would pick the ball up from the defence and we'd begin from there. Teams tried to condense Ossie, they tried to stop Glenn, or push on to me, but we always seemed to wangle our way out of it. There weren't many games when we walked off the field and thought, "Actually, they sussed our game." So it was a system, but it was really all about the players involved.'

At this point, Spurs were still in the FA Cup and jostling for room at the top of the league. It was going to be Tottenham Hotspur's finest season. Sure, 1960/61 had been the Double, but this was going to be the glory days plus one. Yet, if there was a treble, it was one of near-misses. The League Cup was the first to slip out of their hands. They fell to Arsenal eventually in a three-game semi-final. On 18 April against Charlton, Allen might have equalled that Greaves club record of 44 goals in a season, and then taken it from the great man two days later against West Ham at Upton Park, but even so – even though he'd done what he'd told Greaves was impossible – all those goals weren't enough. Spurs finished third in the league behind Liverpool and Everton. When Allen scored his 48th on 4 May in the 4-0 home win against Manchester United, it was already too late. These days you'd kill for third place. But that was then, not now. They'd lost to their bitterest rivals in the League Cup. They'd missed out on the title to the giants of Merseyside. Wembley was going to be their only chance of something to put in the cabinet. No way could they come away from that fantastic season with nothing to show for it.

Coventry City in the FA Cup Final. As far as the Spurs faithful were concerned, it was going to be a formality. True enough, when the teams had met at Highfield Road the day after Boxing Day Spurs had been on the wrong end of the 4-3 outcome, but that was a blip; Coventry had finished seven places below them in the league, a mid-table side; the closest they'd got to Wembley before was losing to West Ham in the semi-final of the 1980/81 League Cup. Tottenham were way above them in achievement and experience. Every time Spurs had played in an FA Cup Final at Wembley they had won it. Seven times in all, starting in 1901 when, as a Southern League side, they weren't even worthy, in the eyes of some, to be there. And when Clive Allen, decades later, scored with his head to notch up his 49th goal of the season with just two minutes on the clock, the fans thought, *Here we go. We'll be bringing home the Cup for the eighth time. It's only 88 minutes away.*

Afterwards, the great John Motson called it, 'The finest Cup Final I've had the pleasure of commentating on.' But there wasn't much pleasure to be derived if you were Spurs. An element of farce had crept in early, with the sponsored Holsten shirts. The club took delivery of two kits, one for the senior squad and one for the youth. With Holsten being an alcohol brand, the sponsor's name was left off the youth kit. When Allen's header went in with two minutes gone and he reeled away to celebrate that goal number 49, it was a celebration in a mistakenly donned sponsorless shirt intended for a youth player, watched by Holsten top brass who were not best pleased. Neither were the Spurs fans when Coventry equalised seven minutes later through their winger, Dave Bennett. He'd wounded Spurs before as a Manchester City player, part of the side that took part in the epic that was the 1981 Cup Final, when his assist for Tommy Hutchison's goal contributed to the drawn first match, and his acceleration in the replay drew the foul from Paul Miller that earned City a penalty. That final ended well for Spurs. This one didn't. Gary Mabbutt might have forced a goal home before half-time to put them back in the lead, but the second half brought Keith Houchen's spectacular diving header. Then the bad thing. Mabbutt tried to block a Lloyd McGrath cross into the box, which 99 times out of a hundred would have gone out for a corner or Clemence would have kept hold of it. This was the one that got away, though only as far as Mabbutt's knee. Not only was it the own goal that lost Spurs the Cup, but it inspired a Coventry City fanzine, *Gary Mabbutt's Knee.*

'It could only have gone in a foot-square part of the goal,' said Allen, 'and it went in there. It was almost one of those things, when we were fated not to win that final.'

That 1987 FA Cup Final should have been a triumphant send-off for Glenn Hoddle, too. It was his last game for Spurs, after 110 goals in 490 first-team appearances. Spurs fans had lived with his impending loss for so long. There had been rumours of his leaving from the 1980/81 season onwards. 'I once rang up Capital Radio,' says Toby Benjamin, 'and they read out my message asking Glenn Hoddle not to leave. I couldn't imagine Tottenham without him.' Now the fans were going to have to. He was off to Monaco, lured there by an unknown young manager called Arsène Wenger. He had scored his last league goal for Tottenham against Oxford United at White Hart Lane on 25 April. 'I remember standing there like anyone else when he took off from his own half,' recalled Allen. 'Peter Hucker, who I'd played with, was in goal, and he was a very, very good goalkeeper – and Glenn left him on his backside. It was a fitting end for Glenn because everything about that goal was absolutely brilliant.'

Meanwhile, in the October of that 1986/87 season, following some embarrassing tabloid revelations about his private life, Pleat stepped down as manager after just one full season in charge. The new man in the job was Terry Venables. And at Tottenham Hotspur the curtain was about to go up on a whole new era of drama.

Schoolboys' Own Stuff

Gascoigne and Lineker

Wembley, 14 April 1991

Paul Gascoigne was prancing around the touchline in triumph, looking as though he ought to be carrying the Cup. Spurs fans were celebrating as if this had been the final, while the Arsenal fans were correspondingly sour, claiming their hopes of another Double had gone because their defence had had an off day. As if Gascoigne wouldn't have breached any defences in the world up to and including a concrete wall. Arsenal 1, Tottenham Hotspur 3 was how the first semi-final to be played at Wembley ended, forever to be remembered for *that* free kick, from 35 yards out and just five minutes in. 'The best free kick in the history of the FA Cup,' said Venables. 'Wasn't bad, was it?' said Gascoigne.

The lilywhite and red halves of north London had never met in an FA Cup semi-final before, and Arsenal had thought their procession to the final was a certainty; they'd only lost once in the league and were on their way to winning the title, whereas after a nothing-much season Spurs had finished up mid-table. But Spurs had Gazza, and maybe George Graham, a manager who didn't make many mistakes, made one pre-match when he'd gone on too much about him, infecting his team with his own worries, instilling fear by telling them what they had to do when Gascoigne had the ball. Maybe he should have concentrated instead on the threat posed by Gary Lineker because, five minutes after giving Spurs the lead, Gascoigne laid off a ball from Paul Stewart to Paul Allen, and a rapid exchange of passes ended with Allen clear on the right from where he released a low ball in towards the most predatory striker in the league. In the confusion inflicted on the Arsenal defence, Lineker put Spurs 2-0 up.

Arsenal heads began to whirl with thoughts of how they could possibly come back from that, but it looked as if they were let off the hook once

Gascoigne was no longer out there to taunt them. It had been touch and go whether he would make it on to the pitch at all, because not much more than a month previously he had undergone abdominal surgery. 'I don't think they took anything out when they operated,' said the watching Lawrie McMenemy, commentating for BBC radio, 'I think they put something in.' But with half-time approaching, Gascoigne had wilted enough for Arsenal to get one back through Alan Smith, and after the restart – with Gascoigne off to convalesce and Nayim on in his place – they thought they were in with a shout at 2-1. Then Spurs hit them on the break, David Seaman letting Lineker's shot slip through his fingers, the sort of shot he would have saved 99 per cent of the time: 3-1 to Spurs, and you wished you could have stopped everything right there. But then you wished a lot of things at the end of a season when it looked as though Tottenham Hotspur was going to go bust.

Wind the reel back through to Venables' first two years at White Hart Lane. Where were the goals going to come from? Who was going to form Tottenham's new strike partnership? Clive Allen was never to repeat his record-breaking season and, in the one that followed, Nico Claesen matched him goal for goal before returning unmourned to Belgium. February 1988 brought the arrival from Liverpool of the talented but combustible Paul Walsh, who had partnered Kenny Dalglish up front in place of an injured Ian Rush and scored 14 seconds into his Anfield debut. There was no doubting Walsh's ability – he had been a PFA Young Player of the Year – but filigree ankles had hampered his progress on Merseyside, as well as a tendency to pick up red cards, and in due course he was to find himself frozen out at Tottenham after banjoing reserve-team manager Ray Clemence for substituting him during a game against Charlton Athletic.

To boost the ordnance up front, Venables paid a top-dollar £1.7m in the summer of 1988 to Manchester City for Paul Stewart, whose 24-goal season had not been enough to lift them back into the top flight. Stewart, though, slipped into town relatively unnoticed because the signing of the summer was a wily cherub-faced handful with galloping ADHD, a low boredom threshold and the ability to plot comic scenarios that rivalled Buster Keaton's.

Paul Gascoigne was all set to go to Manchester United, but when Alex Ferguson arrived back from his summer break in full expectation of welcoming the Newcastle prodigy to Old Trafford it was to discover that Spurs chairman Irving Scholar had hijacked the move, with Gascoigne firmly ensconced at White Hart Lane and his mum and dad house-hunting for the des res that Scholar had promised Gascoigne he would buy for them if he signed for Spurs. If you look back now over the decades that followed, this is possibly the closest you'll get to a Manchester United player being filched by Tottenham rather than the other way round.

With Walsh and Stewart paired up front and Gascoigne expected to amaze and delight in midfield, the fans' hopes sky-rocketed. This was what Venables, the cleverest coach in the country, had been brought to Spurs for – to win silverware. But Gascoigne, and Spurs along with him, made a terrible start to the season. Stewart's debut featured a penalty miss and he went on posing no goal threat in the first ten games. The tabloids were calling

Gascoigne a £2.2m flop and christening Venables 'El Veg'. A week into November 1988 Spurs were bottom of the table after losing 3-1 at home to Derby County.

The turning point came when Gascoigne's form took off and Erik Thorstvedt arrived to replace Bobby Mimms, who had conceded 22 goals in the first half of the season, by which time his name had metamorphosised to 'Booby'. Thorstvedt's debut featured him dropping the ball into his own net against Nottingham Forest, mind. But then Chris Waddle went on to have his best season ever, his 14 goals outnumbering Stewart's by two, and Tottenham recovered to finish sixth in the league. Not that that was where it stopped. The real take-off happened when, in summer 1989, Gary Lineker followed Venables to Tottenham.

Lineker arrived from Barcelona, where he had been a Venables signing and was part of the side that won the Copa del Rey in 1988 and the European Cup Winners' Cup in 1989, but then Johan Cruyff took over as manager and stuck him on the right of midfield, which for someone only interested in scoring goals was where the red line was located.

Lineker had been a Golden Boot winner at Mexico 86 and now he wasn't even an automatic name on Cruyff's team sheet. Joining his former manager at Tottenham was a no-brainer.

John Barnes described Lineker as an out-and-out goalscorer, one who didn't seek perfection by beating a few players and stroking the ball into the net. 'Ultimately for him… it doesn't matter if it goes in off his knee or his bum or whatever,' said Barnes, 'it's still a goal.' Gascoigne, Lineker and Waddle – it was going to be the dream trinity, like Law, Best and Charlton for modern times. With Gascoigne and Waddle feeding Lineker exquisite passes from midfield, this would definitely be the year the league title came back to White Hart Lane.

It was a short-lived nirvana. Just over a fortnight later Irving Scholar announced that Marseille had offered silly money for Chris Waddle. Behind the scenes, the club were waist-deep in financial slurry through a combination of cockeyed commercial decisions and a boardroom that was a roiling mass of competing factions. These were the last days of a regime that had begun so optimistically in the early 1980s with a new board dragging dowdy old

White Hart Lane into a thrilling modern world of superstars, Stock Exchange flotation, rebuilt stands and iconic shirts. Now they were some £18m in debt and the sale of Waddle to Marseille was essential to keep them afloat. 'I didn't want to sell him,' Venables yelped later. Even so, it made sense. The money could be ploughed back into strengthening the team. Except most of it wasn't, it was used to contribute to the cause of extinguishing the binfire that Tottenham's finances had turned into. 'Within six months, instead of buying more players, I was being asked to sell more of the ones we already had,' recalled Venables.

Still, after another faltering start, the 1989/90 season ended up as one of the best for ages. Having scored 12 goals in his first season, Paul Stewart had started firing blanks and Venables made the decision to convert him to midfield, backing up a strike force of Lineker and Paul Walsh. It worked. Lineker didn't really need a partner up front, though, not when he had Gascoigne. Two players who were a cut above the rest of the side, they were the ones who formed the real partnership: attacks beginning with Lineker pulling out wide, stretching the defence, or darting inside with a little burst; a signal to Gascoigne to indicate whether the ball was to be short or long; Gazza delivering. Or the other way round. By the end of the season Lineker's goal tally in the league was 24, and Tottenham had won eight of their final ten games to claim third place behind Liverpool and Arsenal. But how much longer would Gascoigne be around?

As the 1990/91 season unfolded, as Paul Stewart scored in the third round of the FA Cup against his starter club Blackpool, as Gascoigne scored two and made two more in the fourth round against Oxford United – the first for Lineker, the second for Gary Mabbutt – and as he scored both for Spurs in their 2-1 fifth-round win over Portsmouth followed by the winner in the quarter-final against Notts County, the shock news was out. The Midland Bank had placed the club in its 'Intensive Care Unit', a euphemistic way of saying Spurs were hanging from a cliff edge by fingers that the bank were readying themselves to stamp on. Gascoigne was about to be sold to the Italian club Lazio.

While all this was going on, the prospect of Robert Maxwell getting his hands on the club was looming over Spurs. In an attempt to seduce the fans, Maxwell had promised that he would keep Gascoigne at White Hart Lane. Venables, meanwhile, had long cherished an ambition to be the organ grinder, not the monkey, and on the eve of the Wembley final against Nottingham Forest he was in a hotel, desperately trying to put together a consortium to gain control. It still wasn't happening at 7.45pm, when Venables had to join the team. The deal was dead, and 24 hours later the fear was that Gascoigne's career was as well.

Wembley, 18 May 1991

If only Gascoigne had kept his hair on. If only the referee Roger Milford had given him a red card as soon as he'd gone unhinged into that tackle on Forest's Garry Parker. Maybe it was the determination to go out with a flourish, to cram as much as he could into his last performance for Spurs, but the curtain had only just gone up when Gascoigne got stuck in on Parker with a challenge so ludicrously high you wondered if someone had bet him he could reach his opponent's Adam's apple. He got away with it, but the lesson wasn't learned. On the quarter-hour, as the full-back Gary Charles zipped across the edge of the Spurs penalty area, a hurtling Gascoigne scythed him down. What followed was one of the weirdest, hardest-to-compute moments in FA Cup history. Gascoigne got up from the tackle and stood watching Stuart Pearce score from the resulting free kick. Then he collapsed as though his legs were made of wool. He said later that, as he was being stretchered off with a self-inflicted, career-sabotaging rupture to his cruciate ligament, all he was thinking about was who would collect his loser's or winner's medal.

It was a winner's medal that someone collected for him. Lineker might have had a legitimate goal given offside, he might have missed a penalty, but Spurs hung on through the rest of the first half. Gascoigne's goals and assists might have been what got Spurs to Wembley, but now he was done and this day belonged to Paul Stewart. Nine minutes after the restart Paul Allen scurried to meet a ball from Nayim and Stewart raced up on the outside to knock the equaliser in at the post. In extra time Stewart back-headed Nayim's corner across goal, and Des Walker – in order to prevent Gary Mabbutt getting to it – headed it into his own net.

Six weeks after Tottenham's Cup victory, Spurs fans cheered as Alan Sugar and Terry Venables arrived at White Hart Lane for a press conference. Tottenham Hotspur was now under Sugar's control and he would be chairman of a newly formed board that included Venables as a major shareholder and salaried chief executive. The plan was for them to collaborate, with Venables looking after the football side and Sugar taking care of business.

The football side wasn't going so well. Tottenham had been living dangerously in the 1991/92 season, when relegation meant they would not be part of the newly established Premier League. Lineker missed a key part of the season owing to the serious illness of his baby son, returning in time to score the two goals against relegation rivals Luton Town. It was his last season for Spurs and, looking back, arguably his best. His 28 goals in 35 league games had him crowned Footballer of the Year and – more importantly for Spurs – saved the club from the catastrophe of dropping into the Second Division on the eve of the launch of the Premier League.

Ultimately, the arrangement between Sugar and Venables turned out to be unworkable. Sugar's beef was that Venables was treating him as a silent backer who would sit back and bankroll everything while Venables ran the whole caboodle. In December 1991, Spurs had issued more shares under a rights issue, thus allowing Sugar to increase his control of the company to 48 per cent, while Venables – already under pressure financially – could only increase his holding to 23 per cent. The ground was laid for what happened on 14 May 1993, when the Spurs board passed a resolution to remove Venables as chief executive. Not a man to go quietly, Venables obtained an injunction against the board's decision and was temporarily reinstated. The ensuing legal battle gripped the nation, with TV footage of crowds outside the High Court brandishing placards emblazoned with paint-splattered messages such as TERRY IS SWEETER THAN SUGAR, WE WANT T NO SUGAR and ONE MAN'S MONEY AGAINST 27,000 PEOPLES WISHES. The people might have loved Venables but the judge did not. He lost his case and left, later to resurface as England manager. His legacy at Spurs wasn't only that FA Cup, mind.

One of the last players he bought before he went was
Teddy Sheringham.

Walking in a Klinsmann Wonderland

Klinsmann and Sheringham

Hillsborough, 20 August 1994

They'd left the showstopper till last. As one of Darren Anderton's crosses floated into the goalmouth, Jürgen Klinsmann's *pas de chat* threw Des Walker so completely it looked as if he'd got a free header. Goal! It was Klinsmann's first for Spurs, so the only way to celebrate was to wheel away for a full-length dive, and then Teddy Sheringham dived too, right next to his new strike partner, hugging his head.

Sheffield Wednesday v Spurs had been a goalfest all the way through, Sheringham opening the scoring, curling a shot with the outside of his right foot past Kevin Pressman. Another came on the half-hour from a move started by Klinsmann, when Sheringham's no-look pass gave Anderton a free run at goal. Then came one from Nick Barmby, top of the net from Sheringham's back-header. In among all that, Wednesday got two themselves, the second of them when Colin Calderwood swept the ball into his own net after 66 minutes in a desperate attempt to get in ahead of Chris Bart-Williams. The whole thing neatly encapsulated everything that was right and wrong about Ossie Ardiles's Spurs, a side with a defence as impermeable as fishnet and an attack consisting of what would quickly become known as the Famous Five: Darren Anderton, an international-class winger who could cross like Glenn Hoddle; Nicky Barmby, a winger and prodigy only just out of his teens; Teddy Sheringham, a forward and second striker, intelligent, stylish and ageless; Ilie Dumitrescu, a new big-money signing, Romanian World Cup star forward who was upstaged by the most famous of all… Jürgen Klinsmann, the German World Cup hero/villain and so-called diver who, having scored the winner against Wednesday, was stretchered off six minutes from time after clashing heads with

Walker. Klinsmann resurfaced afterwards to charm the media, lisping through a stitched-up lip that he really enjoyed playing in such an exciting game. It was pretty much how he'd charmed them at his first press conference when before they asked him any questions he asked them one of his own: 'Are there any good diving schools in London?'

It was the opening day of the 1994/95 season and Tottenham had been the big story all summer. This was a club that, owing to Sheringham's prolonged outage through injury, had spent most of last season in a firefight to avoid the drop, and they were starting the new one with points already deducted and an FA Cup ban, thanks to sanctions about irregular payments made to players by the Irving Scholar regime. Alan Sugar, the knight in shining armour who had rescued the club from the slavering jaws of the monster Robert Maxwell, was now the baddie who had told Terry Venables to get his coat. Fans had burned their season tickets outside White Hart Lane in protest, their fury barely assuaged by the instalment of Spurs icon Ardiles as his replacement.

You don't become a multi-millionaire businessman by passing up a chance to placate the customer base, though, and Sugar's next move was his most breathtaking yet, signing Klinsmann on his Monaco mega-yacht. 'It was 25 per cent cosmetic,' said Sugar. Klinsmann, a Monaco player at the time, fancied playing in the Premier League, London was his choice of base, and Tottenham got in there in front of Chelsea, Arsenal and West Ham. There was, of course, the drawback that he had been the most reviled man in English football since 1990. His charge sheet included being part of the West German side that beat Bobby Robson's men in the semi-final of that year's World Cup, the offence compounded by un-British histrionics that engineered the sending-off of Argentina's Pedro Monzón in the final and the subsequent penalty goal. TV footage of Klinsmann's masterly goalscoring and melodramatic writhings, and headlines like 'DIVE BOMBER', had accompanied the signing. 'He went down like a sack of coal in one World Cup match. That won't be stood for here. He won't get away with any nonsense,' was the warning posted by former referee Keith Hackett in the *Daily Mirror*. At a pre-season game at Watford, home fans had worn gas masks. He was greeted at

Hillsborough by Wednesday fans gleefully holding up diving scorecards. But if you were Spurs, none of that mattered.

'I can always remember the day,' says the BBC reporter Chris Slegg. 'I was on holiday in Rhodes with my mum and dad and brother, and when you were on holiday you'd buy a paper and it would be a day late. My brother and I were both big Tottenham fans and we spotted the back page of an English paper on the rack outside a beachfront shop. English papers were very expensive, and we had to get some money from our mum and dad, it was probably about five quid on a single newspaper, but the headline was saying that Spurs had signed Jürgen Klinsmann. Tottenham had just stayed up by three points the season before – we were about to start the new one on minus 12 points and now on the back page it's saying we've signed the player who'd won the World Cup in Italy in 1990 when he'd been the scourge of all England fans for his histrionics and his diving, and who a month ago in the World Cup in the US had scored some brilliant goals – and here we are a month after that tournament being told we're going to sign him!'

'It was one of those signings that make you beside yourself,' says Theo Delaney. 'I was so excited. My girlfriend and I were sitting in a traffic jam in Bayswater Road with the radio on when I heard the news. It was a good thing we were in a traffic jam because otherwise I would have crashed the car. I was hyperventilating. We'd lived together for four or five years. She *hated* football. To her it was like The Other Woman. Spurs signed Klinsmann. We looked at each other and I think we both knew. He signed and within six weeks my relationship had split up. Ever since I've had this headline in my head: "JÜRGEN KLINSMANN WRECKED MY MARRIAGE".'

Klinsmann's home debut was a midweek clash with Everton, and is carved so deeply into fans' memories that 23 years later, when the whistle blew on the very last game at White Hart Lane and triggered a mass pitch invasion, there were a handful of fans re-enacting, in almost the same spot, the German's dive celebration after opening the scoring with a bicycle kick. This time the whole side had plunged to the grass, even Ian Walker loping up from his goal to join in. It's all there in *The Team That Dared To Do*, the book Chris Slegg wrote with

Gerry Francis about a season that was a distillation of every Tottenham Hotspur trope of the last half-century: flair football played by extraordinary individuals but undermined by defensive frailties; a managerial sacking; crushed dreams of silverware; the almost comedic denouement and a brilliant strike partnership that in the end brought nothing. But oh boy, it was a lot of fun. It's claimed that two weeks was all it took for replica shirt sales to reimburse Sugar for Klinsmann's transfer fee and salary, and the club shop was reduced to borrowing from Arsenal's stock of letter Ns after their own supply ran short. As the Paxton Road scoreboard put it when it flashed up a German flag, WUNDERBAR JÜRGEN.

For Ossie Ardiles, it turned out not to be that wunderbar after all. In the first six games of the season, Klinnsman chalked up seven goals – unsurpassed for a newcomer – but, even so, Spurs had only nine points to show for it. The goals were piling up at both ends. 'The front is now looking good,' Ardiles had told the press before the season started, 'but don't ask me about the back.' But of course that was all everyone wanted to talk about.

Having won three of their first four games, they lost at Southampton and Liverpool, then at home to Nottingham Forest, and the centre-backs were so exposed they might as well have been asked to beat the opposition into submission with a bunch of daffodils. Not that Ardiles underwent a change of policy. The message to his team remained the same: 'Pass, pass, pass.' 'Everyone was talking about the Famous Five, but no one mentioned us,' said Justin Edinburgh. 'We should have been called the Shit Four.'

They'd been to Maine Road and lost 5-2 to a mediocre Manchester City three days before they rocked up at Meadow Lane for their League Cup third round tie against Notts County, bottom of the First Division and winless at home for half a year. It was 26 October 1994, and Ossie's dark evening of the soul.

'The night… was wet, dark and cold – horrible,' recounted Ardiles in his autobiography *Ossie's Dream*. 'When we arrived at Meadow Lane with Tottenham and all its stars I remember feeling that it was a recipe for disaster.' Spurs had already conceded twice in the first half when Dumitrescu got sent off and the ten men still standing lost 3-0. Fans were banging on the sides of the team bus as it left Meadow Lane, shouting 'We want Ossie out.' Sugar had sat in the directors' lounge afterwards, simmering. 'They slaughtered us and made us look stupid,' he recalled in *What You See Is What You Get*. 'This was the final straw.' Ardiles, he concluded, would have to go. Klinsmann, Sheringham and Barmby put three past West Ham in the league the following Saturday, but the die was already cast. Sugar sacked him on the Sunday. 'ARDILESS' was the *Guardian* headline on Monday. Sugar 2, Managers 0.

As Gerry Francis took over, defensive stability returned to the team with the simple exercise of bringing back the midfielder David Howells, who had been overlooked by Ardiles. They notched up their first clean sheet of the season in a 0-0 home draw against Chelsea and went on to win six out of their next nine games. While all that was going on, a court case overturned the points ban for irregular payments in favour of a hefty fine and, more importantly, rescinded the FA Cup ban. Just in time for the third-round draw to take place.

They got Altrincham, the well-known giant-killing Cup minnows, but dispatched them 3-0 at White Hart Lane, no problem. Next up was Sunderland. It was a mere four days after Klinsmann had been knocked unconscious again, this time in a collision with Aston Villa's keeper, Mark Bosnich. The first time, the collision with Des Walker at Hillsborough, had been purely accidental. About this one, he had some doubts. The doctors told him that it had been a matter of inches – a few more either way and the impact would have killed him. Now he was scoring two at Roker Park and his strike partner the other in a 3-1 win that took them into the fifth round. There their opponents, Southampton, put up more of a fight. It ended 1-1 at White Hart Lane (Klinsmann the goalscorer, obviously). In the replay at The Dell, Spurs were 2-0 down at half-time, with the fans bracing themselves for defeat, when Ronny Rosenthal came on as a sub and scored twice in as many minutes to take the tie into extra time. Rosenthal then got his hat-trick and Sheringham, Anderton and Barmby added three more.

They'd started the season already out of the Cup. Now they had a big chance of bringing it back to White Hart Lane. Then came the draw for the next round. Fans' hearts sank. A Cup quarter-final at Anfield. They would be facing the Liverpool of Ian Rush, Robbie Fowler, Steve McManaman and John Barnes. Spurs would have no chance. You didn't go there and win if you were Tottenham Hotspur.

Theo Delaney was in Italy on the day of the match. 'I was watching Milan v Padua at the San Siro, and Milan didn't need to break sweat – it was a boring game. So I went back to my hotel and put the telly on – and there was Spurs v Liverpool live from Anfield! *Whaaat?* It was the encapsulation of what made Klinsmann and Sheringham great. End of the first half, Klinsmann assist, Teddy hits the most perfect clipped shot. Pure class. The confidence. The way the two embrace. Klinsmann scores the winner. Two minutes to go. Teddy, beautiful little flick in the box. Klinsmann on it like a panther. I'm going mad in an Italian hotel room.'

It looked as if this was going to be a year when Spurs won the Cup, but then they met Everton at Elland Road and were ushered out 4-1 by Joe Royle's hard men. Klinsmann scored Tottenham's goal – not that it was much consolation – but that quarter-final performance stayed in Sheringham's mind. It was, he said later, one of the standout memories of his career.

'Klinsmann and Sheringham together became a world-class partnership,' enthuses Delaney. 'I was going home and away and I felt Sheringham was very inhibited at first by playing with a superstar, but Klinsmann worked with him, told him he was a top, top player and could wreak havoc. A few games into the Gerry Francis regime, it started to happen. Suddenly Teddy took the leap and became a number 10 and a better player. He played with such joy. You could imagine him thinking, *I've never played with anyone this good before!* Klinsmann *elevated* Sheringham.'

Klinsmann would have concurred with at least some of that. 'It was a fantastic partnership – so much fun,' he said in a 2007 interview in *The Tottenham Hotspur Opus*. 'He was the most intelligent striker I ever worked with. I felt so comfortable with that group of players I probably ended up playing the best season of my career.'

'Jürgen was 31 when he first joined Spurs,' said Sheringham later, 'but sometimes he was like a kid playing football in the park, galloping about with his blond mop and scoring goals. You gave him half a chance from anywhere and more often than not he would hit the target. He was just ridiculously good.'

Klinsmann might have clicked with Sheringham on the field but his closest friendship at Tottenham was with Gary Mabbutt. A smart person, he said: 'He looks beyond the normal football horizon.' It was Mabbutt he confided in when he made the decision to leave at the end of the season. 'That won't go down very well,' Mabbutt told him with classic understatement. But when signing for Spurs, Klinsmann had insisted on a one-year get-out clause in his contract. Sugar had agreed – with the proviso that it applied only in the event of Spurs being relegated. Unfortunately for Sugar, that hadn't been put in writing. With a month of the season left, Klinsmann duly broke the news that he would shortly be off to join Bayern Munich, suggesting that as a token of thanks for adhering to the get-out clause he would offer Sugar a signed shirt. Offered one during a subsequent *Sportsnight* interview, Sugar threw it at the reporter, saying, 'I wouldn't use it to wash my windscreen.'

Ossie Ardiles had picked Klinsmann up from the airport when he arrived, and was the last to see him before he left England. He offered to drive him to the airport but Jürgen said he was going on the bus.

Nobody would have put money on it then, but he'd be back.

Postscript

It was almost inevitable. The partnership with Klinsmann had put Sheringham on a level where he became one of England's most highly rated strikers. Together, their goal tally was 53 in all competitions and 39 in the league, and for one extraordinary season they were the best strike partnership in England. The way they worked together – Klinsmann the out-and-out goalscorer, Sheringham making the play – set the template for striking duos in the years to follow. Yet, in a career spanning 15 years, Sheringham had never won a major trophy. He was now past 30 and in 1997, with the time to redress that issue diminishing, he left for Manchester United.

'Without doubt Sheringham learned so much from Klinsmann,' says Chris Slegg, 'and he went to another level, a level which in the end saw him taken away from us. Every summer it was, *Is this the one when he's going to go?* and ultimately he was prised away. Manchester United were easily the best team in the 1990s. He went on to win the Treble with them and he was certainly a player worthy of those top, top prizes.'

Sheringham and Klinsmann might have been regarded as *the* strike partnership, but when in July 2023 the BBC Sport website listed the top ten duos in Premier League history for combined goals and assists, it was Sheringham's partnership with Darren Anderton that featured at number five, above more lauded pairings such as Mo Salah and Roberto Firmino, Freddie Ljungberg and Thierry Henry, and Robbie Fowler and Steve McManaman:

'Even with Teddy Sheringham moving to Manchester United for four seasons and Darren Anderton's well-documented injury problems, the pair still managed to forge a very productive partnership at Tottenham. In seven seasons, split over two spells, the duo used all their vision, skill and guile to pick open defences, combining 27 times for goals, with Sheringham netting the vast majority of those (20). Their peak as a partnership came at the start of the 1994/95 season, with Anderton providing six assists for Sheringham in the first half of the league campaign. They also played together 15 times for England, most notably throughout Euro 96 as the Three Lions reached the semi-finals on home turf. Sheringham's second departure from Spurs in 2003, to join Portsmouth, ended their playing relationship, with Anderton leaving the club a year later to join Birmingham.'

Of course, like Klinsmann, Sheringham would be back, but a lot was to happen before he wore a Spurs shirt again.

We Want Our Tottenham Back

Klinsmann and Ferdinand

Old Trafford, 10 January 1998

The bookies were offering odds of 13-2 against Tottenham winning and you'd have been nuts to hand over your money. They had started the year 19th in the league and – even with Jürgen Klinsmann making his comeback that day – Spurs weren't going to get anything at Old Trafford. 'THE GREAT DIVIDE' blared the front-page splash on the *Sunday Telegraph* sports section the next day: 'Old pals Klinsmann and Sheringham meet at Old Trafford but their teams head in opposite directions'; and what had gone on that afternoon showed why. Manchester United 2, Tottenham 0 was how it finished. 'It was a win, that's all,' said

Alex Ferguson afterwards. 'I think we were just too comfortable. We were in second gear a lot of the time.'

The return of Klinsmann to Tottenham had been huge news, though this time instead of being cast as Football's Most Hated he was accorded the status of honorary national treasure, profiled elsewhere in the *Sunday Telegraph* as 'England's favourite German'. Why had he come back to join a football club that was facing relegation was the question posed by the journalist Helena de Bertodano, and he answered that it was out of nostalgia and a sense of duty: 'It was a special year for me and I feel responsible for helping to get Spurs out of this situation.' he said. There were, of course, additional incentives: £30,000 a week and the guarantee that he would start every game. At 33, he was still in with a chance of making it into the Germany squad for the upcoming World Cup but, having been benched after falling out with his manager at Sampdoria, he figured that a return to Tottenham would give him enough playing time to ensure he made it to France. To which end, reputedly, he had it stipulated in his contract that he would not be left out of the Spurs side. Along with that, it was rumoured that he was to have a say in tactics and team selection.

The *Sunday Telegraph* interview provided at least one significant demonstration of Klinsmann in action. The Tottenham training ground was besieged by a multi-national press pack and there was no press officer to deal with them. 'Are you responsible for this mess?' one shouted to Klinsmann. 'I am never responsible for mess,' he responded, and organised them into a five-minute briefing session: 'You will have to approve which questions you want to ask together. Otherwise it will take the whole day.'

In fact, he was clearly back at Tottenham to organise the team as well. At Old Trafford, he had preceded his manager into the press conference. 'We are in big, big trouble now,' he admitted. 'West Ham have beaten Barnsley 6-0 today, so next week we have kind of a final.' It was Jürgen Klinsmann who was in charge now.

Before this goes any further, an update. After Klinsmann finished his first stint at Spurs in 1995, he was replaced by Chris Armstrong, for whom

Crystal Palace were paid a fee of £4.5m, top dollar back then for a young player who everyone hoped would do well but was still comparatively unproven. 'No disrespect to Chris Armstrong,' says Chris Slegg, 'but Sheringham's been scoring goals for fun, the whole team's been scoring goals for fun and, let's face it, it's going to be very hard for anyone to follow in Jürgen Klinsmann's footsteps. It never really worked for Chris Armstrong and it was a source of frustration for all the fans. Down the road they'd signed Dennis Bergkamp and I remember fans singing, "Armstrong is better than Bergkamp," and feeling I really couldn't join in with that chant.'

Meanwhile, Nicky Barmby had left for Middlesbrough that summer too. Ilie Dumitrescu was offloaded to West Ham the following January and, with Sheringham gone, the Famous Five was down to a Famous One: Darren Anderton. With Sheringham's departure leaving the team one striker short, Alan Sugar went shopping. At Newcastle, Kenny Dalglish had replaced Kevin Keegan as manager, and the warrior Scot regarded David Ginola as too much of an ornamental luxury. The deal that brought Ginola to Spurs was conducted on board the yacht in Monaco that had been the setting for Klinsmann's signing three years earlier, Ginola arriving from his home in St Tropez by speedboat as only Ginola could.

Along with the French superstar, Spurs welcomed another of Dalglish's cast-offs, Les Ferdinand. At Tottenham today, there is still big love for Sir Les, who went on to be part of the coaching set-up at the club after his playing days were over. Yet, in the summer of 1997 – having spent two seasons on Tyneside and collected runners-up medals in the Premier League under Kevin Keegan's management – he was, like Ginola, considered surplus to requirements. Tottenham was the club of Ferdinand's boyhood, and Gerry Francis had been his manager at QPR, so a move back to London made sense. At least until he set foot in White Hart Lane. 'Tottenham was a club in unbelievable turmoil and I didn't realise how bad it was till I got there,' said Ferdinand in a later interview with the Newcastle United magazine, *The Mag*. 'In my first five years I had four different managers and a change of board, so that tells you the type of turmoil the club was in.'

Ferdinand was to score twice on his debut against Aston Villa, but then injuries sabotaged his progress. By early October 1997, Spurs had won just two out of ten games. On the terraces fans were shouting, 'We want our Tottenham back.' After losing at Anfield – they conceded four in the second half – Francis resigned, saying he felt he'd lost the support of the dressing room. His successor, Christian Gross, arrived from Switzerland that November. Impressed by the success of Arsène Wenger, a French coach largely unknown in England until he took over at Arsenal, Sugar had decided to go down the same route.

The appointment was a disaster. Gross's first press conference in front of a xenophobic English media didn't help. He might have taken Zurich Grasshoppers to two Swiss championships, but any curiosity the red-top press had about what was going on in Europe stopped well short of Switzerland. Not only had they never heard of him but at his introductory press conference he guaranteed himself mickey-taking in perpetuity for the London Underground travel card that he waved at the reptiles that constituted England's football press with the bathetic comment, 'I want this to become the ticket to my dreams.'

Some hope. From his first day in the role, Gross was up against it. His fitness coach and right-hand man, Fritz Schmid, was denied a work permit. The players found it difficult to understand Gross's guttural accent, hated the hard and relentless training regime, and ridiculed fussy rules such as his insistence that players were not to fold their arms while he was talking to them, and that they had to use placemats and napkins in the canteen.

Tottenham were 16th in the league when he took over, one point above the drop zone. Below them were Everton and Bolton, who each had a game in hand. Gross's first game in charge was at Goodison, a much-valued 2-0 win. Significantly, though, the scorers were Ginola and the centre-back Ramon Vega. Gross's first home game featured a 6-1 defenestration by Chelsea, Vega again the goalscorer. Spurs didn't have a strike partnership that worked.

'To play in a traditional strike pairing at that time should have been any centre-forward's dream, with Anderton and Ginola on the wings providing world-class delivery,' points out the Spurs commentator Gareth Dace. 'But in Ferdinand, Armstrong and Iversen we were left with a mismatch of centre-forwards where no two really complemented each other. Armstrong had been bought in 1995 as a natural complement to Sheringham; Steffen Iversen had been signed for his raw potential in December 1996, with a view to playing alongside Sheringham, and Ferdinand was an expensive panic signing once Sheringham had departed. Manchester United, who famously won the Treble in 1999, rotated their four strikers – Yorke, Cole, Sheringham and Solskjær – which kept opponents guessing before and during games. They could rotate from a position of strength, but for Spurs the constant rotation was a problem. Iversen and Armstrong was the most commonly used combination, and there were brief experiments with just one striker playing and even one game where all three started. None of them were able to hit any sort of form and only on two occasions through the whole season did two of them score in the same game.'

Small wonder that everyone greeted Klinsmann's return with enthusiasm; everyone, that was, except Gross. 'Jürgen proved too big a character for him to handle,' said the former left-back Justin Edinburgh, speaking in 2007. 'Then we had Les Ferdinand and David Ginola voicing their opinions too. He didn't know how to deal with players talking back to him. It took away his power. There were meetings among players. Jürgen was certainly holding court, and an idea to go against the manager and do it our own way was discussed, and to an extent that happened.'

'He's given everyone a huge morale boost,' Gary Mabbutt had told the *Sunday Telegraph*. 'It's not just because he's probably still one of the best strikers in the world, but also he's a catalyst on the field. He helps to bring out the best in other players – things happen around him.'

What happened next was that Klinsmann scored the winner against West Ham but pretty soon after that he broke his nose against fellow league strugglers Barnsley in the FA Cup fourth round (Spurs lost) and that was him out for precious weeks at the same time as Ferdinand was crocked. Spurs were beginning to concrete themselves into the relegation zone, their only comfort being that the teams around them were even worse. By the time they met Newcastle in late April they had registered one win in their last seven games, but at last Klinsmann and Ferdinand were able to start together up front. It was Ginola who made the breakthrough for the opening goal, roaming around the middle, apparently shifted wide out of danger by Warren Barton, then suddenly turning to cross for Klinsmann to score with a downward header. Then 17 minutes from the final whistle Ginola's corner gave Ferdinand the chance for him to head home his first club goal for seven months.

The following week, against Wimbledon at Selhurst Park, the pair provided the goals that saved Tottenham. The opener came from Ferdinand: a Ginola shot hitting an upright, Anderton picking up the rebound on the right and crossing for Klinsmann, who headed down to Ferdinand inside the six-yard area. Ferdinand wasn't going to miss from there. Nothing was ever easy, of course; Wimbledon fought back from being a goal down to taking a first-half lead until Klinsmann levelled just before half-time, Ginola sweeping past Ben Thatcher to deliver a pass that Klinsmann chipped inside the far post. Shortly afterwards, Thatcher was red-carded for flattening Allan Nielsen, and in the second half Klinsmann just went turbo. Three goals in five minutes, the first made by Nicola Berti, the other two by Ferdinand. The sub Moussa Saïb added another to make it Wimbledon 2 Tottenham Hotspur 6.

In two games within a week of each other, the Klinsmann–Ferdinand strike partnership, with a bit of help from Ginola, had saved Tottenham from dropping out of the Premier League. They didn't need points in their final game, at home to Southampton, but it finished 1-1, Klinsmann scoring his last ever goal for Spurs.

Postscript

While Tottenham were saving themselves from the drop, another club that had had its fair share of glory in the past was finding itself at its lowest ebb for 111 years. Manchester City, league champions in 1968 and winners of the European Cup Winners' Cup in 1970, had been relegated from the Premier League in 1997. Now their season had finished with them dropping down for the first time ever into the third tier. At that point, no one could have dreamed that, 12 years on, these same two clubs would be battling each other for a tilt at the biggest prize in Europe.

Gareth Bale, He Plays on the Left

Crouch Plus One

Eastlands, 5 May 2010

'Blue Moon' blasting into the twilight, the Eastlands floodlights so powerful they were probably visible in Wigan, and a crunch match that turned out to be a play-off for the last spot in the top four. Whoever came off best would arrive at a place neither Spurs nor Manchester City had ever been, their *Ultima Thule*, that distant unknown region known as the Champions League.

A win for City would serve the ambitions of the squillionaires who had bankrolled them all the way out of grotty Maine Road after years as the poor relations of the mob across town. As for Spurs, it had been 48 years since they had played in the

Champions League's forerunner, the European Cup, and victory here would mean the world. Charlie Watts once said that life as a Rolling Stone was 50 years in the band – ten spent drumming and the other 40 waiting for something to happen. Spurs hadn't hung around that long but it had been ages since they were really something. And they had to wait a bit more because it took a chalked-off Ledley King goal and 82 minutes before Younes Kaboul went raiding along the right, sashayed past Craig Bellamy's challenge and got in a cross. Márton Fülöp parried it but only to Peter Crouch, who outjumped Vincent Kompany to head home.

Crouch had only signed for Spurs at the start of that season, but it was a repeat experience: his first pro contract with them was in 1998 when he was just out of the youth team. He got nowhere and left two years later for a peripatetic career that included QPR, Aston Villa, Southampton, Liverpool and Portsmouth before fetching up back at White Hart Lane in the summer of 2009. At Eastlands that night his partner up front was Jermain Defoe, but it could have been Roman Pavlyuchenko, Robbie Keane or Darren Bent, while the fact that his goal was scored

144

with an assist from a right-back hinted at the pattern to come. It was Tottenham's most important goal in modern times, and Crouch hadn't needed a regular strike partner to accomplish it.

Things had happened on Tottenham's road to the 2010/11 Champions League that are part of club folklore. They had been rattling on the door since Martin Jol's spell as manager. On the last day of the 2005/06 season a falsely accused lasagne – the villain of the piece turned out to be norovirus – left them with incapacitated players just when they needed a win against West Ham to secure fourth place. They lost, and Arsenal leapfrogged over them to claim it. Jol went on to be sacked in the most jaw-dropping manner possible in October 2007, halfway through Tottenham's 2-1 defeat to Getafe in the UEFA Cup, when everybody in the ground knew it was about to happen except him.

His replacement, the grim-faced Juande Ramos, prodded them to a trophy, the 2008 League Cup, and you'd have thought they would have gone on from there. Instead, Ramos lost the dressing room and Spurs cratered, bottom of the table after amassing two points from their first eight games and inspiring a joke about Oxo creating a cube in their honour. It was called Laughing Stock. Ramos was told to clear his desk. His replacement was the genial Harry Redknapp, someone who would put an arm around his players, who immediately lifted the mood. He motivated everyone. In their 2010/11 season Spurs played a front-foot 4-4-2 with wingers most of the time; they had the insanely good Luka Modrić in midfield, an inspired last-minute signing in Rafael van der Vaart, and a strike partnership that was usually Crouch and a plus-one. It's normally a dominant pair up front that makes the difference, but instead they had Gareth Bale.

Moved to the wing to accommodate Benoît Assou-Ekotto at left-back, Bale became the breakout star of a Champions League run that nearly hit the buffers in Tottenham's opening tie on a plastic pitch against Young Boys of Bern in the group-stage play-off. 'If we turn up we'll be fine,' Clive Allen had said. As first-team coach, he had scouted the opposition, but for most of the first half Spurs, in their hastily purchased astroturf boots, were anything but fine. They were 3-0 down before the half-hour point, and it could have been 4-0 except Moreno Costanzo sent a free kick only just over the bar. 'I thought you said they were useless,' Redknapp said to Allen, but then came the fightback, with goals from Sébastien Bassong and Roman Pavlyuchenko narrowing the gap to 3-2. Bullet dodged. They won the return leg 4-0. Bale was Crouch's plus-one for two of the beanpole striker's goals that night, and he won the penalty Crouch scored for his hat-trick. Defoe's goal was also down to Bale's work. Spurs had made it through to the group stage.

A football reporter is meant to embrace detachment, but to a Spurs fan like me that first Champions League season meant weeks of partisan joy. At the end of September, it was the Dutch side Twente Enschede at White Hart Lane in the pouring rain. Pavlyuchenko and Crouch were up front, and the Twente fans were chanting 'You're shit and you know you are' to their compatriot Van der Vaart, who metaphorically two-fingered them with a sensational goal before missing a penalty and getting sent off after two yellow cards. Meanwhile, Spurs were awarded a second penalty. The Russian now known as Superpav scored it, and then another, before Bale wrapped up a 4-1 win in the 85th minute.

But the ties that are memory-banked are the ones that followed against an Inter Milan side whose line-up included Javier Zanetti and Maicon, two of the best defenders in the world, Walter Samuel, one of the top centre-backs of his generation, and up front Samuel Eto'o, a man who had already scored in two Champions League finals. This was, in short, a side that knew what winning at the highest level tasted like. The first leg was at the San Siro, and an immediate nightmare; Inter were frighteningly good in the first half, turning over the Spurs defence time and time again, leaving Spurs 2-0 down in an 11-minute burst of horror in which goalkeeper Heurelho Gomes was sent off. After 14 minutes it was 3-0 and by the 35th minute it was 4-0 and could have been more.

Four goals and a man down – how do you come back from that? Tim Sherwood, assistant first-team coach, was urging Redknapp to take Bale off, save him for Everton at the weekend, shore it up so it doesn't finish six or seven, but Redknapp would have none of it. Win this half so it doesn't turn into a rout, he told the players. The whole world's watching, play for pride, give it a go.

What followed was one of the greatest comebacks football has ever witnessed. The opening minutes of the second half, you couldn't believe Spurs had a prayer, the way Inter were stroking the ball around. Then Jermaine Jenas broke up an Inter attack and the ball fell to Crouch who laid it off for Bale, deep in his own half. And Bale just *went*. The pace and the power were extraordinary; no defender on earth could have stopped him. It was his star-is-born night, the night he left Zanetti, Maicon and Samuel for dead, a 50-yard run down the left and a finish that flew past Júlio César. Fast-forward to the 90th minute when Bale got his second and it was almost a re-run of his first, tearing past Zanetti again; his third came almost straight from the kick-off, when Aaron Lennon put him through. Bale 52; Bale 90; Bale 90+1. From 4-0 down to 4-3 – they'd lost but it felt like a win. They belonged at this level.

The comeback had got into Inter's heads. Two weeks later at White Hart Lane, Van der Vaart scored clinically from a ball by Modrić and then Bale set himself alight again. This was the 'Taxi for Maicon' night of legend, when Bale tore the

Brazilian to pieces on the left flank. 'Get it to Gareth at every opportunity,' Redknapp had said, though this time when Bale got it he made goals for the others: the plus-one for tap-ins from Crouch and Pavlyuchenko.

A comeback to 4-3 and a 3-1 win at White Hart Lane. You barely had eyes for any other player than Bale, but at the end of November when Werder Bremen came to White Hart Lane and left defeated, it was goals from Kaboul, Modrić and Crouch that clinched a place in the last 16. Two weeks later winter had set in with a vengeance when, on a bone-freezing night in Holland, Defoe came up with a brace and the Twente Enschede keeper with a comedy own goal to register a 3-3 draw, meaning Spurs finished top of their group.

In the knockout phase, Spurs drew AC Milan, bringing a return to the San Siro in the New Year. With Bale out injured. Crouch, though, was around to score the only goal of the game, Aaron Lennon his plus-one that night, moving down the right at Bale-like pace to square a ball for Crouch to sweep home. There was a hint of a scuff about the shot, but who cared?

Every fan has a favourite moment. I'd thought mine was Bale scoring his 91st-minute third against Inter almost from kick-off but, looking back, it was the head-to-head between Joe Jordan, Redknapp's assistant manager, and the venerable Milan midfielder Gennaro Gattuso that filled me with childish glee. They'd had words on the sidelines already after Mathieu Flamini's two-footed slam tackle on Vedran Ćorluka when, as the game continued, a bit of a push and a shove culminated in Gattuso raising his hands to Jordan's throat. Then at the final whistle Gattuso decided to pursue his point. Jordan – now a balding, greying, bespectacled 59-year-old, but once a striker for Leeds and Manchester United so feared he was known as Jaws – calmly took his glasses off and handed them to a member of the Spurs bench. Gattuso attempted a half-hearted headbutt before he was taken away. 'I don't know why it got so silly,' mused Redknapp later. 'Gattuso obviously hadn't done his homework. He could have picked a fight with anybody else.'

Three weeks on, in the return leg, AC Milan turned up with three men up front and dominated most of the play. It took a William Gallas goalmouth clearance and brilliant organising of the back line to stifle the Italians, but Spurs had done it: they were through to the last eight. It's where that wonderful, joy-filled run ended, of course, against a terrifyingly strong Real Madrid, managed by José Mourinho and packed with all the stars: Iker Casillas, Sergio Ramos, Pepe, Ricardo Carvalho, Marcelo, Xabi Alonso, Sami Khedira, Ángel Di María, Mesut Özil, Cristiano Ronaldo and Emmanuel Adebayor, who only needed five minutes to head in the opening goal. Nine minutes later, Crouch was sent off for a second yellow card. Spurs were still only 1-0 down at half-time but it ended up 4-0. Ronaldo's goal decided the second leg.

It was the end of Tottenham's Champions League story for a while. That season they finished fifth in the league. The one after that saw them finish fourth ahead of Chelsea, who promptly went and won the damn thing, which meant automatic qualification in the following season's tournament at Tottenham's expense. I can still clench my fists at the monumental unfairness of it all. Meanwhile, Modrić went to Real Madrid in 2012 and Bale followed him in the summer of 2013.

Spurs weren't done yet, though. Bale, like Hoddle before him, was a generational talent, the kind that you only get every so often. And now there was another one on the way, someone whose goals would put Spurs back in the Champions League. All Harry Kane needed was a strike partner.

On Wings of Son

Kane and Son

Tottenham Hotspur Stadium, 7 December 2019

Spurs had won the game against Burnley pretty much before half-time. Only four minutes had gone by before Son's pass gave Kane the chance to whip a 35-yarder past Nick Pope, and then it was as though everything had been speeded up: a shot from Son that Pope got a foot to, but only to send it pinging off Ben Mee for a flick-on by Dele to Lucas Moura at the back post, making it 2-0 in the opening nine minutes. And then *that* goal, on 32 minutes, out of almost nothing. You can still see Son in your mind's eye: Jan Vertonghen hooking a Burnley free kick clear under pressure from James Tarkowski, which was all that was needed, because the ball fell to him just outside the goal area. Son just set off, evading seven Burnley players over 90 yards in 15 unbelievable seconds of running with the ball that ended with his right-footed finish past Pope.

Spurs scored five that day. Nine minutes into the second half, Dele played the pass to Kane that resulted in his 25th goal for club and country that season, and there was a nifty one-two between Kane and Moussa Sissoko for the seldom-on-the-scoresheet French international to finish things off. But Son's was the show-stopper, the one that everyone remembers. He was the last player to leave the pitch, drinking in the applause. In the post-match presser, José Mourinho called him Sonaldo.

I was burrowing back into the records to find out the moment when Kane and Son really took off as a strike partnership when I realised that Spurs v Burnley game in the run-up to Christmas 2019 featured four out of five of the main characters in the Tottenham psychodrama going on around that time – Kane, Son, Dele and Mourinho. The missing one was Mauricio Pochettino, whose sacking on 21 November brought the installation of Mourinho as his replacement. It turned out the Special One's low-block, counter-attack style was perfect for two ultra-intelligent players with hair-trigger reactions and the ability to develop a rapport. I've never been a great fan of managers who centre themselves in the story, but I'm prepared to give Mourinho this; he set the conditions for a strike partnership that four years on would be acclaimed as the greatest in Premier League history.

A lot had to happen before that, of course. Rewind to the summer of 2014. When he took over at Tottenham from Tim Sherwood, Pochettino inherited two front men. There was the quixotically brilliant Emmanuel Adebayor, a star at Arsenal, Manchester City and Real Madrid but now knocking on a bit at 31. Alongside him was the likeable Roberto Soldado, whom Tottenham had broken their transfer record to sign from Valencia in 2013, after which he managed to hit the net six times in his debut season, only twice from open play. By 2 November that year, when they were away to Aston Villa, Spurs had acquired just 11 points from their first nine games and Pochettino was concerned for his future. The visit to Villa Park, it followed, was a must-win, but they were a goal down at half-time. Even though Christian Benteke was red-carded for a shove on Ryan Mason, even though Spurs were starting to control the game, they couldn't break down the ten men remaining. With the clock ticking down, Pochettino turned to his coaching team. 'Pack your bags tonight,' he said, 'because tomorrow we'll be going home.'

But it so happened that ten days previously Spurs had beaten Asteras Tripoli 5-1 in the group stage of the Europa League. A raw, still chubby Harry Kane had scored his first professional hat-trick, as well as heroically going in goal for the final three minutes after Hugo Lloris had been sent off (it was Kane who conceded Asteras Tripoli's solitary goal, mind). The 21-year-old had been out on loan four times and, frustrated after failing even to make the bench against West Bromwich Albion three days later, he went to see Pochettino. He deserved, he thought, to play more. 'You aren't the finished article,' Pochettino had said. 'You need to work on your technique and fitness,' but he could see the determination, the football intelligence and capacity to learn, and now, as a last throw of the dice, he took off Adebayor and sent Kane on. With six minutes left, Nacer Chadli equalised from a corner, but the best was yet to come. On the 90th minute, Spurs were awarded a free kick, and Kane scored from that.

Looking back, the moment Kane came on for Adebayor was symbolic – it was the handing over of the baton. Then, towards the end of that month, Soldado scored his first goal in open play that season, the decider in Tottenham's 2-1 home win over Everton. When he was taken off later in the game, Soldado was given a standing ovation from fans who had sympathised with his endless but unrewarded efforts to come good. That standing ovation seemed symbolic, too; a farewell.

The speed with which Kane not only supplanted him but also became the pre-eminent striker in the Premier League was extraordinary. On New Year's Day 2015, Spurs hosted Chelsea at White Hart Lane. Once Liverpool at Anfield had been the prospect that made the fans cower; now it was Chelsea, a club that – thanks to the largesse of Roman Abramovich – had been carrying off all the available silverware by the sackload. In those days Tottenham never beat Chelsea, except this was the day they did. Chelsea were in pieces by half-time, 3-1 down. Now the world beyond N17 could see where Kane was heading. His first goal – it would become a Kane trademark – was a long shot from 30 yards out. His second just seemed to come out of him lurking unobtrusively on the edge of the box, and then *boom*, the ball was in the net. The eight-year-old boy who had been binned by Arsenal for being too chubby, who between 2011 and 2013 had been loaned out to four clubs, was acting on Pochettino's advice and was hungry, eager and increasingly honed. That season's goal tally was 31, with 21 of them in the league, goals that took Tottenham to a fifth-place finish and brought Kane the award of PFA Young Player of the Year. One more push and Spurs would be back in the Champions League spots. What Kane needed now was a partner up front.

Sometimes you wondered how it would have turned out if the Saido Berahino transfer had gone through. A speedy handful of a centre-forward, Stoke City's Berahino had combined well with Kane on Under-21 international duty and looked ideal. But the whole thing turned into a saga and everything collapsed on transfer deadline day, a thwarted Berahino expressing his chagrin on social media by announcing he would never play for his chairman again.

For Spurs, though, any frustration was short-lived. In the 2014/15 January window they had signed Dele Alli from MK Dons and then loaned him back to his starter club for the rest of that season. A teenaged central midfielder who couldn't stop scoring, Dele was cheeky and creative, mild-mannered off the pitch but on it full of chutzpah and aggression, wandering between the back three, finding space between the channels.

Now, as the 2015/16 season unfolded, and Spurs became challengers at the top of the league, Pochettino had two young players who complemented each other: a killer in the box and an imaginative attacker who could also find the places that goals came from, a pair who were already being called a modern-day Gascoigne and Lineker. That season, Dele assisted seven of Kane's 21 goals, the most from one player to another in Europe's top five leagues. Before Kane and Son, it was Kane and Dele who were *the* strike partnership.

But while Dele was taking the world by storm in that 2015/16 season, and while Spurs were clinching their place in the Champions League, another summer 2015 signing was passing under the radar. Son Heung-min, a midfielder-forward for whom Tottenham paid Bayer Leverkusen £22m, had just turned 23. He came with a reputation as a versatile, two-footed attacker, someone who could play on either wing or up front as a striker if needed.

That season he wasn't needed, not really. In September, he made his debut away to Sunderland and was subbed after 62 minutes. A week later, his first Premier League goal was the winner against Crystal Palace, prompting an impressed Graeme Souness to observe, 'Tottenham might have got themselves a player,' but after that Son started only 13 league games and scored only four goals. One of them was a cracker, mind: he went on as a late substitute against Watford, a backheel, no-look nutmegging of keeper Heurelho Gomes.

As Spurs challenged Leicester for the title, with Kane and Dele between them racking up the goals with the help of Christian Eriksen, Son was finding it tough to force his way into a first XI of rising stars while he was still adjusting to the demands of the Premier League. This was a season spent in the shadows. On the final day, when Spurs lost 5-1 at Newcastle and slipped to third behind Arsenal, he was subbed at half-time. Wolfsburg were ready to take him back to Germany. He asked Pochettino for permission to leave to get more game time and had to be convinced that he was still important and that he should fight for his place.

On 10 September, his first appearance of the 2016/17 season, Son scored twice and created a third goal in Tottenham's 4-0 win over Stoke City. A fortnight later, he scored both goals in their 2-1 victory away to Middlesbrough, thus equalling his previous season's total in 25 fewer games. 'Son is a different person now,' Pochettino commented at the time. 'He knows the league and he's settled in fantastically.' His huge popularity in Asia had him dubbed the David Beckham of South Korea, but in England he was still in Kane's shadow. In the 2018/19 season, though, the plates shifted. For key parts of it, Kane was out injured, and during this time Son came into his own – the hero the team needed. When Spurs moved into their new stadium after two years at Wembley while White Hart Lane was demolished, he was the one who scored the first professional goal on opening night in the 2-1 win over Crystal Palace. When the draw for the last eight of the Champions League took place, it was inevitable that Manchester City would be Spurs' opponents, because they had run away with last season's title and were about to do the same again. The Champions League run was fated to end right there because that was how things always worked out for Spurs. Except this time it didn't. Maybe City were spooked by the new stadium, maybe Lloris saving Sergio Agüero's first-half penalty kick 12 minutes in was what messed with their heads, but – even with Kane limping off after 55 minutes – Spurs held on and in the 78th minute Son dodged Fabian Delph to make it 1-0 with his left foot.

City were still very much in it, though. No one thought a one-goal lead would be enough, especially without Kane. I watched the return leg at home with my family, and it was one of the most bonkers games ever. There was no Spurs strike partnership to speak of, just Son and, on the bench, Fernando Llorente, the ex-Swansea City oldie who had good-naturedly sat out the season as a spare part for the strike machine. There were four goals in the first 11 minutes, Raheem Sterling putting City 1-0 up, then two quickies from Son, then one from Bernardo Silva. It was 3-2 to Spurs on aggregate, and then Sterling scored again.

On the edge of half-time, Sissoko had to hobble off. Instead of sending on another midfielder, Pochettino went for broke and summoned Llorente from the bench. Spurs were hanging on now. With 59 minutes gone, Agüero put City ahead. Then, 15 minutes after that, Llorente was in the right place at the right time to equalise with a shot that bounced in off his hip. A Champions League semi-final was within Tottenham's grasp.

But then, in added time, Sterling got the ball in the net for his hat-trick. As he wheeled away in triumph while the City fans exploded with joy, my furiously disappointed husband switched off the TV and we stomped upstairs to bed. Early the next morning we had a phone call from one of our sons. It was to congratulate me on Spurs winning a place in the semi-final. In our pique, we had missed the VAR decision that Sterling was offside.

I'll be brief here. At the Tottenham Hotspur Stadium, Ajax won the first leg of the semi-final

1-0. The second leg, in Amsterdam, was one of the greatest nights in Spurs' history. Ajax were 2-0 up within 35 minutes. Spurs now needed to score three to go through to the final, and Lucas Moura – with an immense performance by Dele as his strike partner for two of them – duly obliged. Then, even more briefly, Spurs lost to Liverpool in the final in Madrid. A few months after that, Mourinho was the new manager.

* * *

'You're a fucking lazy guy in training.'

Someone had to make way for Kane and Son to happen and it was Dele, trying to forget his troubled childhood with the painkillers to which he had become addicted, his talent numbed and draining away. My favourite goal of their partnership is the one Kane set up for him in the North London Derby in April 2017. The tension had been unbearable during the goalless first half. Whenever play swept towards Spurs' goalmouth I was unable to look, fixing my gaze instead on the sinister gap at the corner of the North and East Stands, freshly cleaved to accommodate the incursion of the new stadium.

Even more was at stake than was normal for this fixture – this would be the first time Spurs had finished above Arsenal since 1995, and the end of all those jibes about St Totteringham's Day, which always infuriated me more than they should have done at my age. No way would we let them have any bragging rights whatsoever. Only a few minutes of the second half had passed when, my heart beating so hard everyone around me must have been able to hear it, I knew I had to get up and move around before I exploded.

I squeezed along the row of seats but, as the crowd noise rose in a crescendo of anticipation, I paused at the top of the steps and turned to see it: Kane to Dele, Dele to Eriksen, back to Dele and… *goal!* Fighting my way back through a jungle of wildly flailing limbs, I just had time to sit down before I was up again to cheer as Kane, tripped by Gabriel Jesus, made it 2-0 with a penalty.

The following year had brought the 2018 World Cup in which Dele and Kane flew high. Now, less than 18 months on, here was the newly appointed Mourinho telling him in a staged one-to-one on *All Or Nothing*: 'I think one day you will regret if you don't reach what you can reach. You should demand more of yourself.'

Mourinho wasn't the only one saying Dele had become lazy. A lot of fans were on his case. No one guessed that for some time those troubled childhood memories and a painkiller addiction had been overwhelming him. As Kane and Son were breaking records, as the Mourinho era imploded and morphed via the brief and unlamented term of Nuno Espírito Santo into the melodrama of Antonio Conte's spell as Spurs manager, Dele was on his way to Everton and then – when that didn't work out as planned – a loan to the Turkish club Besiktas. That didn't go well, either. So in 2023 he returned to Everton, the truth behind his decline revealed in an extraordinary, heartbreakingly honest interview with Gary Neville. Now everyone is hoping that this marvellous player can reconnect with the spirit and hunger that at one point made him one of the best young talents in England.

Postscript

At Elland Road on 26 February 2022 Spurs beat Leeds United 4-0. The final goal was set up by

Kane with a long diagonal pass from the right to Son, who took a touch to enter the box then lashed home a shot. It was another classic from the Kane and Son playbook and meant that, with 37 goal–assist combinations, they had beaten the record held by Frank Lampard and Didier Drogba to become the deadliest strike force in Premier League history.

By then Mourinho had gone, but once again the fans were prepared to accept a managerial replacement associated with deadly rivals Chelsea and renowned for a rigid, often tedious style of football because he was a winner, and in that first season under the excitable Antonio Conte, Spurs regained their Champions League place. It was thanks to the most Kane and Son game ever, the one when their double act almost won the North London Derby on its own. Each was a foil for the other, Arsenal so busy keeping an eye on one that they lost track of what the other was up to. Cédric Soares was reduced to pushing Son in the back as they both went for a Dejan Kulusevski cross, and Kane scored, low and right, from the resultant penalty in the 21st minute. When Kane put Spurs further ahead 16 minutes later, it was from a Son corner from the right, flicked on by Rodrigo Bentancur. Kane was first to the far post for a close-range diving header.

Rob Holding's continued attempts to put Son out of contention earned him a red card. Within an hour, Spurs had a three-goal lead when Kane got the better of Gabriel Jesus, feeding in a ball for Son to fire into the net. And so it stayed till the end. It was Tottenham's longest unbeaten run over Arsenal since the 1960s, when the Double side was king and the G-Men were in their pomp, and the fact that Spurs had stolen fourth place from Arsenal made it all the sweeter.

And then came a season that no one really wants to remember, interrupted by a World Cup in the wrong place at the wrong time, and in which all the bad things that happened seemed to be the bad things that always happened. In February 2023 Conte underwent surgery in Italy, handing over responsibility to his uninspiring assistant Cristian Stellini. Form plummeted. Conte made a brief return to deliver a rant against the players, board and club mentality, and in March 2023 was sacked, leaving Ryan Mason to step in as interim manager again.

And then one more thing happened that hadn't happened before: Kane left.

Some stats, courtesy of the BBC website in July 2023:

'With 47 goal and assist combinations, Kane and Son are the top strike partnership since the start of the Premier League. Of their 47 combinations, Son edges it on goals with 24 to Kane's 23. In a prolific two-season period – 2020/21 and 2021/22 – they linked up 21 times for goals. Kane provided all the assists for Son's four goals at Southampton as they combined for nine goals in five games at the start of the 2020/21 campaign. Kane and Son are now way out in front of their nearest challengers and closing in on 50 goal combinations.'

Kane had delivered, as always. As of July 2023, he had scored 213 goals in 320 Premier League appearances. In each of those nine seasons he scored between 17 and 30 goals. But Kane and Son never did make it to 50 combinations. In September 2023, with the transfer window on the brink of closing, came the announcement that everyone knew was going to happen but tried to close their ears to anyway. Kane was now a Bayern Munich player.

* * *

Turf Moor, 2 September 2023

It's a sunny afternoon in Lancashire and Spurs are running riot. As it's Spurs, nothing is ever simple – they concede early to a goal by Burnley's Lyle Foster. But after two seasons of Antonio Conte's tedious, rigidly defensive football, Ange Postecoglou's Spurs are a joy and a revelation. There are summer signings on show. James Maddison, the magic man in midfield, looks to be the creative playmaker Spurs have craved since Christian Eriksen left for Inter Milan. Guglielmo Vicario has taken over Lloris's long-held spot in goal. Manor Solomon is a lightning winger, while Micky van de Ven is a young giant in central defence next to Cristian Romero, himself a relative newcomer. There's an obvious caveat – it's early days yet. Even so, this promises to be thrill-a-minute, front-foot stuff, players licensed to express themselves, fans singing 'We've got our Tottenham back.' Spurs have opened the season with a 2-2 draw at Brentford, with goals coming from Romero and Emerson Royal. They've followed that up by beating Manchester United 2-0 at home through Pape Matar Sarr and a Lisandro Martínez own goal.

Son is playing central striker today and the way he and Maddison are finding each other, it looks as though they've played together for years, but right now it's Pedro Porro who releases a long ball forward from right-back to set up Son's equaliser, a dink past James Trafford. Next it's Romero's turn to score, from 25 yards out into the top corner, making it 2-1 at the break, but in the second half Spurs start going through the gears. Maddison curls a shot home to make it 3-1 and from then on it's Son's game all the way; Solomon sweeps in a ball for his second of the afternoon and a through-ball from Porro sees him complete his hat-trick at the near post. Burnley 2 Tottenham 5.

I wondered for a long time what the title of this chapter should be. I did think about 'The Greatest Pair In History' but decided it sounded a bit rude. In the end I chose a pun. 'On Wings of Song' is a lyric poem set in bygone days to music by Felix

Mendelssohn. The original is soppy stuff – 'On wings of song I'll bear thee, / My heart's love, far away' – but you get the picture. I thought of the way Son has carried Spurs through all the ups and downs of the last few years. Always smiling, always running, he has been everything that is decent and dedicated about football, not just as part of one of the greatest strike partnerships in history but the hero Spurs needed when things looked bleak, because it was never just about one man. Not even if he was Harry Kane.

Epilogue

I'M HEADING out of Seven Sisters station and along the High Road when I realise the pointlessness of what I'm doing. The object of the exercise was to conjure up in my imagination what it must have been like in 1961, on that April night against Sheffield Wednesday, but as the saying goes, you can't swim in the same river twice. Even if the old White Hart Lane pitch were still there, it wouldn't be the same pitch. Within hours of Bobby and Les scoring the goals that won the title, the grass would have been cut, divots replaced, lines repainted. Heaven knows how often it had been made over by the time the G-Men came along, let alone when Crooks found the net against league champions Nottingham Forest as he and Archibald made their debuts in August 1980. Or that evening in 1994, home to Everton, when the whole team dived to celebrate alongside Klinsmann, or the evening Bale scorched down the flank against Inter to leave Maicon a broken man. Or indeed New Year's Day 2015 when Kane's goals against Chelsea marked the start of his legend.

All that remains of that pitch now is a commemorative plaque on the South Stand walkway that marks the centre spot. That and a few clods of grass pilfered by fans when everyone invaded the pitch after the last game ever to be played at the Lane. Spurs beat Manchester United 2-1, with goals by Victor Wanyama and, inevitably, Kane. I don't know if anyone's still tending these mementos. My friend and sometime co-author Rob White buried his in the gravel in the front garden of his new house for confused archaeologists to scratch their heads over at some point in the far future.

Writing this has been a bit like archaeology too. Even the relatively recent past quickly becomes distant. I was there in 2019 when Son scored the first professional goal at the new Spurs Stadium but, although I remember that game emotionally – the joy I felt for Son, the angst that somehow Crystal

Palace would still find a way to win remaining unassuaged till the final whistle had blown – I had to dig out old reports and clips online to remind me of the details.

I stand at the corner of Park Lane and Worcester Avenue and study the aerial photo on my phone. The old stadium is on the left, still intact, but the new one, a work in progress, is poised to consume it, a Jaws made of steel and brick. It triggers the memory of Kane and Dele against Arsenal, young guns going for it while I was so hyped up I could hardly bear to watch and had to stare at that gouge in the corner of the ground where a slice of the North Stand has been taken away.

Another jump backwards in time, another building site. In my head it's now 1980, and there's flat earth where the old West Stand once rose. At home games you would often see the odd builder standing on top of a pile of rubble, watching the action. And what action it was. Being asked to name your favourite strike partnership is like being asked to choose between your children, but my memories of Archie and Garth are particularly fond; two super-bright young strikers who miraculously

176

clicked with each other to take Spurs back to the top.

Now in my mind's eye the old West Stand has magically rebuilt itself, and the teenage me is sitting high up in it, watching the G-Men against West Ham. The ticket was given to me by Ron Greenwood, who lived four houses away from my parents; I had cosied up to him at a neighbours' cocktail do, telling him how much I loved football, particularly West Ham. Both Jimmy and Gilly scored that day, along with Terry Venables, but West Ham won 4-3. I had to pretend to Mr Greenwood that I was in raptures about the result.

But the Double season is almost prehistory for me. One of my few claims to fame is that I once wrote a film, *Those Glory, Glory Days*, about a little gang of 12-year-old girls who followed Spurs all the way through the Double season. I'm still often asked whether it was autobiographical. Some of it is, some isn't. The reality is that I was too young to be allowed to go to football when goals from Bobby Smith and Les Allen clinched the 1960/61 title. The Double season for me meant the sports pages of my parents' *Daily Telegraph*, augmented by surreptitiously bought copies of the *Daily Mirror* and *Daily Sketch* (my mother didn't approve of such working-class rags) outside Loughton station on my way to catch the tube to school.

Mining the newsroom in the British Library for those old reports was both a happy and slightly morbid experience. The owners of the bylines on those reports have now departed for the great press box in the sky, and 60 years from now – who knows how people will consume their news by then? – I'll be long gone too. But maybe another writer will want to find out what the great double act of Kane and Son did back in the mists of time, in which case I hope my words will provide the assist.

The lovely part was that it brought my childhood passion for Spurs back into sharp focus, and with it the confirmation of the huge and essential part Smith and Allen played in that great Double side: opening the season together with a goal each against Everton... Smith's early-season hat-trick against Blackpool that broke the club scoring record held by George Hunt since 1938... the pair of them bagging braces against Blackburn Rovers at the end of the year. Two of the best strikers in history, unmatched in their harmony, each a foil for the other, as 60 years later Kane and Son would be. What terror they must have instilled in the hearts of the opposition. And here they are now in the photos, as vividly invincible as they were in real time: Bobby with Danny Blanchflower, leading the lap of honour at Wembley, holding up the FA Cup; Les hanging over the side of the directors' box at White Hart Lane, waving a towel as a banner, wild with happiness. Smith and Allen, towering goalscorers, the only double act I never got to see but always my favourite, because they were the first.

About the Author

JULIE WELCH is an award-winning author and journalist who was the first woman to report football for a national newspaper, the *Observer*. As well as writing for most national newspapers, her work includes the film *Those Glory, Glory Days*, about the Spurs Double-winning side of 1960/61, *26.2: Running the London Marathon*, the hardback best-selling *The Ghost of White Hart Lane* (with Rob White) and the critically acclaimed *The Fleet Street Girls*.

She is also the author of *The Biography of Tottenham Hotspur*, first published in 2012 and now in its fourth edition, and quite coincidentally shares a birthday with Spurs, although of course she is not quite as old.

Outside of football, her main interest is running. She has finished six London marathons and many more off-road, although her greatest athletic feat remains the completion of the Long Distance Walkers Association's annual Hundred, a gruelling non-stop 100-mile walk which she would not have contemplated doing had a publisher not paid her to write about in *Out On Your Feet*.

Her most recent book is *81: The Year That Changed Our Lives*, co-written with legendary Spurs captain Steve Perryman and short-listed for the Sunday Times British Sports Book Awards 2023.

FOOTBALL SHORTS

2023 marked the successful launch of the series, with three great books …

Pantomime Hero
Jimmy Armfield
*Memories of the man who
lifted Leeds after Brian Clough*
By Ian Ridley

The Homecoming
The Lionesses and Beyond
By Jane Purdon

Blue was the Colour
A Tale of Tarnished Love
By Andy Hamilton

**All available individually for £9.99 each,
signed by the authors, or £25 for the set of
three at www.football-shorts.co.uk.**

And 2024 heralds another terrific trio of superb short reads ...

After *Double Acts*, May will see the publication of *Namasté, Geezer* by Shekhar Bhatia, respected and experienced journalist who has covered countless World Cups and Olympic Games as a news reporter for national papers. Shekhar will write about what it was like growing up in the East End of London loving West Ham – and having to run from his own supporters.

September will then mark the release of the brilliant David Winner's perceptive and incisive analysis of Gareth Southgate's tenure as England manager, how he changed the mood of the national team, and how it all panned out at Euro '24. David, the author of such classics as Brilliant Orange and Those Feet, will place the Southgate reign in the context of the nation's social and political landscape.

Each of this year's books – signed by the author - can be ordered from Football Shorts at £9.99 or £25 for the set of three. Just go to www.football-shorts.co.uk or scan the QR code below, or on one of the inside covers of this book, and head to our shop.

In fact, why not set up an annual direct debit of £25 and we will send you all books, signed? Just click on 'Annual Subscription' in our shop.